FLIP YOUR LIFE

FLIP YOUR LIFE

How to Find Opportunity in
Distress—in Real Estate,
Business, and Life

TAREK EL MOUSSA

with *Jonathan Leach*

hachette
BOOKS
NEW YORK

Hachette Go, an imprint of Hachette Books
Hachette Book Group
1290 Avenue of the Americas
New York, NY 10104
HachetteGo.com
Facebook.com/HachetteGo
Instagram.com/HachetteGo

First Edition: February 2024
Published by Hachette Go, an imprint of Hachette Book Group, Inc. The Hachette Go name and logo are trademarks of the Hachette Book Group.

The Hachette Speakers Bureau provides a wide range of authors for speaking events. To find out more, visit hachettespeakersbureau.com or email HachetteSpeakers@hbgusa.com.

Hachette Go books may be purchased in bulk for business, educational, or promotional use. For information, please contact your local bookseller or email the Hachette Book Group Special Markets Department at Special.Markets@hbgusa.com.

The publisher is not responsible for websites (or their content) that are not owned by the publisher.

Print book interior design by Sheryl Kober

Library of Congress Cataloging-in-Publication Data

Name: El Moussa, Tarek, 1981– author.
Title: Flip your life: how to find opportunity in distress—in real estate, business, and life / Tarek El Moussa.
Description: First edition. | New York: Hachette Go, [2024] | Includes bibliographical references.
Identifiers: LCCN 2023034879 | ISBN 9780306830877 (hardcover) | ISBN 9780306830884 (trade paperback) | ISBN 9780306830891 (ebook)
Subjects: LCSH: El Moussa, Tarek, 1981– | Flipping (Real estate investment)—United States. | Businesspeople—United States. | Success in business. | Success.
Classification: LCC HD259 .E326 2024 | DDC 332.63/240973—dc23/eng/20230810
LC record available at https://lccn.loc.gov/2023034879
ISBNs: 978-0-306-83087-7 (hardcover); 978-0-306-83089-1 (ebook); 978-0-306-83545-2 (B&N signed edition); 978-0-306-83547-6 (signed edition)

Printed in the United States of America

LSC-C

Printing 1, 2023

This book is dedicated to my family. To my wife, kids, and parents, who gave me the drive to accomplish what many said was impossible. I couldn't have done it without you.

CONTENTS

PROLOGUE Return on Investment **ix**

CHAPTER ONE Locate **1**

CHAPTER TWO "Flipping 101" **13**

CHAPTER THREE Evaluate **21**

CHAPTER FOUR Emulate **39**

CHAPTER FIVE Prepare to Launch **53**

CHAPTER SIX Enlist Your Crew **71**

CHAPTER SEVEN Duplicate **93**

CHAPTER EIGHT Renovate Relentlessly **109**

CHAPTER NINE Dream Big **125**

CHAPTER TEN Remember the Basics **145**

CHAPTER ELEVEN Take Massive Action **159**

CHAPTER TWELVE Doubling Down **173**

EPILOGUE Closing the Sale **189**

APPENDIX **197**

ACKNOWLEDGMENTS **215**

NOTES **217**

ABOUT THE AUTHOR **223**

PROLOGUE

Return on Investment

I got started flipping houses the hard way: I worked my ass off, got my ass kicked a few times, and then figured out for myself what worked and what didn't. It wasn't the most efficient approach to learning, but I knew what I needed to do to succeed—because I had lived it. That's the difference between "school learning" and street learning. Street learning never lets you forget. Sure, you can read how to ride a bike. Or you can get out in the street, crash a few times, and bleed a little bit. After you crash, you definitely know what not to do. Next thing you know, you're riding. That's pretty much how I got started flipping: by crashing a few times, bleeding a little, and just doing it!

Frankly, I never thought I would be alive long enough to do this book. In the part of Orange County, on the Los Angeles border, where I grew up, the surrounding neighborhoods were influenced by gangs, and more than once I found myself in situations where I was lucky to come out alive. After I graduated from high school, I started college classes, but college wasn't for me. I felt so lost, so directionless and depressed, that I "self-medicated" with a bottle of vodka, plus beer, every night for almost a year. Once I established myself in the real estate business and became a top producer, the 2008 Great Recession came along and nearly wiped me out. When I was still in my early thirties, I was diagnosed with two different cancers, and I thought for sure I was a dead man. One cancer? That seemed beatable somehow. But two? No way. I thought my life was over.

After I finished my cancer treatments and went through some miserable back surgery, I was ready to put my focus back on my businesses and on *Flip or Flop*, the hit TV show that had taken my then-wife, Christina, and me to amazing heights. Then our marriage began to crumble, in a very public way. Our breakup and eventual divorce were tabloid headlines for years. When I wasn't on the set filming the show, I was hiding from the paparazzi and grieving the end of our marriage.

Today, I'm more alive than ever and my health is great. I'm excited about the future and I have more energy than I've ever had. I'm having more fun now managing my three-ring circus of TV shows, investment deals, and training programs than I ever could have imagined. Make no mistake: there's a lot of pressure, and I'm still in the spotlight. If I "flop," my flop is going to be seen by millions of people. But no matter what happens, I know I'll figure out the "flip": I'll find a way to find the good inside the bad and turn disaster into opportunity. In other words, I'll do what I've been doing all my life: going all in until I find success.

It's all about embracing the Flip Your Life mindset: always looking for ways to pivot, to find a path that can take you to the next level, and then *taking massive action*. It's about looking for that window of opportunity and then running through it.

Disappointment and misfortune come to all of us, but I'm convinced that all of us have what it takes to come back. Flipping your life means not just thinking about doing it, but *actually doing it*. You have to make a commitment to flip your life, over and over again. You have to accept the challenge of renovating yourself relentlessly and trying to improve every single day.

Many things inspired me to write this book. One of them is a comment I've heard from many people over the years. People say it differently, but the gist is the same, and it sounds something like this: "Tarek, you know all these people and you have these great contacts. You can make a deal happen by picking up the phone." When I hear that, I know this person assumes I was an overnight success, and it happened by magic.

And I think, *If you only knew what I've been through. If you only knew my "before," not just my "after."* Here's one example, ironically enough involving my contacts! One of the biggest "flops" in my life was when I lost my entire list of contacts—my sales book of leads that I had spent months putting together. Losing that sales book destroyed my business and left me with no prospects and no money. I had to flip that situation in a hurry—which, in my case, involved walking across a parking lot in Cerritos, California. As you'll learn, that short walk was the beginning of a flip that changed my life forever. It's just one part of the story I've been wanting to tell.

Something else that inspired this book is the work I've done and the deals I've made in nearly fifteen years of flipping houses. I can't help noticing the similarities between what a successful house flipper does, in the world of bricks and mortar, and the things that all of us can do in our personal lives to have the best possible shot at happiness.

In both cases, it starts with a vision. What does the future look like? Once you finish the remodel, how much will your investment be worth? As a flipper, you know you've found the right house when you're confident you can sell it for more—hopefully, a lot more—than what it will cost you to buy it and renovate it. When you think about that future value, you don't need to be precise and down to the penny. In fact, you can't be. So many things can happen, and so many variables come into play, that it's impossible to know exactly how much a house flip is going to cost you. That's the reality of flipping houses, and it's a major premise of my TV shows. Nasty surprises happen, and you have to deal with them. But *big dreams are more powerful than setbacks.* Big dreams inspire you to take action, and they keep you going when things turn bad and you feel like quitting.

There's something intuitive about big dreams. You might not be able to express them in words, but you sure feel them in your gut. Starting out as a young real estate agent, I did the "expected" things, the things new agents are supposed to do. I studied what agents around me were doing, and I did my best to do those things. I held open houses, I passed out hundreds of flyers, and I waited for the phone to ring. But deep down, I knew there had to be a better way. The dream I had for myself was bigger—much bigger. In my gut, I knew what I was doing wasn't going to get me there. At the time, I might not have been able to put all of this into words. All I knew was that I had to get busy. I had to find a path to that bigger vision.

The challenge I faced was that no one I knew could show me that path. I had questions, but I had to go find the right people to answer them. That meant getting out of the safe, comfortable environment of that real estate office. I had to go knock on doors, and reach out to people, and show up, and *keep at it*, until I understood what to do next. Once I understood what to do, I took massive action. Yes, there were disappointments and setbacks. That's life. But eventually, as you'll learn, I started to have success. My plan started working. And with every success, I gained the confidence to set my sights even higher.

Along the way, I learned that action creates opportunity. The idea I had for a TV show—the spark that became *Flip or Flop*—was a crazy idea. At the time, Christina and I didn't know the first thing about flipping houses, let alone being on television. But I had a powerful hunch that people would watch a show about flipping houses. And my big dream inspired action. As soon as I understood what steps to take, I went all out to create that opportunity for us.

Here's another parallel between flipping a house and renovating your life. In one word, it's *urgency*. Flippers have to move fast, or else they go broke. In a typical deal, a flipper buys a house by using a hard-money loan—a short-term loan with a higher-than-average interest rate. That means that every day that house is unsold, the flipper is paying a lot of money for it. Their outgoing expense is huge, and their income is zero. So a flipper has to get that house renovated and sold, and they need to do it fast.

The same urgency applies to flipping your life. Time is our most valuable resource, and if you waste it, you never get it back. This is true for everybody, without exception.

Personalities and temperaments vary from one person to the next. I get that. For example, it's obvious to me that not everyone has the right temperament for flipping houses. Not everyone has the high tolerance for risk, or the sense of "hurry up," that flipping demands. But I also know that the built-in urgency of flipping houses suits me. Speaking for myself, I tend to get frustrated with how long everything takes. I wish things would go faster, and I feel like I'm always battling time. For as long as I can remember, I've brought a sense of urgency to everything I do.

But when it comes to flipping your life, we're no longer talking about temperaments or preferences or personality types. No matter who you are or where you are in life, you must come up with an exciting vision that will propel you to the next level. Then you must take action to realize your dreams. You can't just sit there thinking about what you want to do. *You must go do what you want to do*, and never look back. Take it from someone who has had more than one brush with death: the clock is ticking. Starting now, you must chase your dreams.

Speaking of urgency, here's something else I've learned from flipping close to a thousand houses. Successful flippers don't cheat, but they do take appropriate shortcuts.

To be successful, a house flipper must deliver a safe, high-quality product to a buyer. As they're rehabbing a house, flippers don't patch over a defect. If the sewer line is faulty, they fix it. If there's a problem with the electrical wiring, they fix it. They get it done. They don't ignore problems that may affect the safety and well-being of the people who will be living there. The flipper's honesty and integrity are on the line. Sadly, there are shady operators out there who do it differently, but those flippers don't last long. Word gets around, and the cheaters go broke. Cheaters never win.

The same principles apply when you decide to flip your life. You can't cheat. You can't cheat by risking your health or safety, or disregarding your loved ones, or putting things off that you know are important. You can't cheat by lying to yourself and pretending you're not responsible for what happens in your life. You must take ownership of your own outcomes.

But there's working hard, and there's working smart. The key is to do both at the same time.

Successful flippers don't try to reinvent the wheel. Yes, their goal is to offer a house that is clean and safe and attractive. But on the way to that goal, successful flippers do the best they can with what's already there. They take appropriate shortcuts. And the fundamental shortcut is: Control the things you can control, and acknowledge the things you can't.

Think of it this way. Suppose you're flipping a house, and you know that by knocking out a particular wall, you could open up the "flow" of that house and create a much bigger family room. All you need to do is knock down that wall. Then you find out that the wall is load bearing. If you knock down that wall, you'll destabilize the structure, and the whole house might collapse.

This is where the "shortcut" comes in. Sure, that load-bearing wall can be moved—if you've got the time and money to do it. For that matter, any problem you discover in a house can be solved, if you throw enough money at it! But you're a flipper, not an architect or builder. You're in the business of buying, rehabbing, and selling homes, not doing major surgery on them. Meanwhile, the clock is ticking. Every day that house isn't sold, it's costing you money. You need to minimize the bleeding by making quick decisions and moving fast. You have to stay focused on your overall goal: a house that is clean, safe, attractive, and profitable, *on time and within budget.*

Maybe the shortcut is leaving that wall in place, *and* finding a way to make it work. Maybe you hang a huge painting on it, or you turn it into an accent wall. Over time, as your business grows and you're making more money, you learn other shortcuts on the way to that overall goal of a safe and profitable flip. Maybe, like me, you hire contractors to do the things you used to do yourself. Maybe you take a course that teaches you how to find those contractors. Instead of trying to be your own interior designer, maybe you take the shortcut of learning how to find the best designs.

Flipping your life means being as smart as you can, and working as hard as you can, as you chase your dreams. If it's about improving your health and getting in better shape, seek out the people who have the answers. Instead of pretending you have all the answers, go see a doctor, or work with a trainer or a nutritionist. Be persistent about asking questions: How do I lose weight? How do I get healthier? Get help figuring out what you can control, and what you can't. Whatever your personal flip looks like, the moment you know what to do next, move fast and go all out.

———

I've framed *Flip Your Life* as a blueprint for success. Drawing on my personal life, my twenty years of experience in the real estate business, and the images and vocabulary of the house-flipping world, I'll lay out the roadmap that has led me to where I am today. I'll share the steps I've taken—steps that anyone can take—to create the best chance for prosperity and happiness. To help you get started on your own path to success, I've included some exercises to work through in the appendix at the end of the book.

As I say, there have been some serious missteps and roadblocks in my journey. I've written this book to be a candid, nothing-held-back, up-close-and-personal "tell-all" of my life. It's a story filled with crazy twists, terrifying downturns, wild victories, and dumb mistakes. I firmly believe that my stumbles, my triumphs, and my unique platform give me some insight worth sharing.

You might as well know: there's someone else I've written this book for, and it's me. In writing this book, I've tried to keep the younger Tarek El Moussa in mind, Tarek as I was twenty years ago. That person was less experienced, more anxious, more self-critical, and way more unhappy than the Tarek I am today. I hope this book is one that my younger self would have eagerly read and absorbed as a kind of training manual for life.

Just as in the house-flipping realm, there's a recipe for success. There are learnable, easy-to-implement habits and strategies that can help you position your life in ways that will enable you to flourish. When you're willing to do the work, and *you do it*, you give yourself the best chance to move toward the life you've dreamed of—and surpass it. So…what are we waiting for? Let's get started.

CHAPTER ONE

LOCATE

When Ronnie and I arrived home and saw that the landlord had bull-dozed our apartment, we figured he was sending us a message.

It was the fall of 2000, and since the day we'd graduated from high school just a few months earlier, we'd been renting a unit in a run-down triplex in Newport Beach. The place seemed perfect for two young Southern California bachelors. Sure, it smelled a little funky, and there was barely enough room for the battered couch and bunkbed we'd bought off Craigslist. It probably wasn't an ideal environment for us to be studying in—if we ever decided to study. But as Ronnie pointed out, there was one feature that completely outweighed those minor issues: the apartment was just steps from the ocean. And our prized bodyboards fit nicely next to the front door, in easy reach.

Then the nightmare began. Just months after we moved in, a new owner bought the building, and he planned to remodel and raise the rent. This new owner made it clear that Ronnie and I were not in his plans. He

1

wanted us out. We refused. On his last visit, he tried to convince us that because of the change in ownership, our lease was no longer valid. Clearly, he thought we were stupid. True, we were either intoxicated or asleep a good part of the time. But we weren't stupid. And we consistently paid our rent.

"We're not leaving," I told him. "We have a lease."

Now we'd come home from class to discover that our entire unit had been demoed. An exterior wall had been completely taken down to the studs. Our kitchen was gone; our bathroom was gone; there was debris everywhere. Chunks of drywall littered the entire place. To me, it felt like we were in a movie—it couldn't be real. Plainly visible from the street, and exposed to the elements, was our little bunkbed. For a minute or two, Ronnie and I stood there on the sidewalk, taking it in. Then we lost it. Ronnie started the rant first. He was tall and redheaded, and his vocabulary was as colorful as mine. Of course, I immediately joined in. Rage, grief, and anger came tumbling out in long strings of four-letter words. Then we stumbled inside—or, more accurately, what used to be inside. Everything we owned was buried under the rubble and covered in drywall dust. Almost all of it was damaged.

As we shuffled through the wreckage, neither one of us said it, but we were both thinking it: *What do we do now?* Obviously, this was no longer a livable home. Equally obvious was that the owner now assumed he had solved his problem: us. He thought we would be gone forever. But Ronnie and I had a bigger problem: neither of us had anywhere else to go.

"Screw it," I said. "We're not going anywhere."

So we hunkered down in that ruined shell for another month. It was a pathetic and strange and desperate month. At night, we would lie there in the bunkbed, looking through the wall studs, watching cars drive by. All we had for warmth was a little 1970s wall heater that threatened to burn our eyebrows off every time we tried to light it. One day, while Ronnie and I were in class, thieves walked in and helped themselves to most of our things, including our prized bodyboards.

Meanwhile, my mind was in turmoil. I had no doubt that Ronnie and I were in the right. The owner had clearly violated our lease. But another part of me was in panic. For all of the anger I felt toward our landlord, I was just as angry at myself for the way my life was going. The landlord may have bulldozed my physical space, but I was already doing a great job of destroying the rest of my life all by myself.

I had graduated from Sunny Hills High School in Fullerton. As an athlete, I'd worked out every day during high school, and it had showed. At Sunny Hills, I'd always been a leader. I'd excelled in sports and was pretty popular. Frankly, I had always gotten anything I wanted. Suddenly, in college, all of that was over. Graduation was supposed to mean moving on with your life, choosing an exciting major or pursuing some other big dream. Not for me. After just a few months, my life was starting to feel like a total disaster.

When Ronnie and I had moved into the triplex, I'd had no idea who I was or what I wanted to do. Yes, I was taking college classes here and there, but I absolutely despised them. Ronnie and I took odd jobs to pay the rent, but they were jobs with no future. Meanwhile, I couldn't stop thinking about what it had been like to be fit and motivated. Now I weighed 235 pounds and had gone completely downhill. In a matter of months, I had gained 55 pounds. I had put the pounds on so fast that there were dark purple stretch marks on my new love handles! To get my shorts on, I had to use an elastic hair tie as a "button extender" on my waistband. I was so ashamed to be shirtless that I quit doing anything outdoors. It was obvious to me that I was no longer The Man—just a guy who was fat, sad, and drunk, sitting on a couch alone. At nineteen, I had become The Guy Who Used to Be The Man.

And every time I looked in the mirror, I hated myself.

AMERICAN DREAMS

I'm confident that when my parents fled their bombed-out Beirut apartment and immigrated to the United States in 1978, they never imagined that a child of theirs would one day be living a bombed-out life in sunny Southern California, in an apartment with no kitchen, no bathroom, and only half a wall.

My mom was born Dominique Arnould in Belgium. Blonde and pretty and eager to see the world, she was barely out of her teens when she took a job as a flight attendant for a Belgian airline. One night in Cairo, she went out with her crew for drinks at a spot not far from the pyramids. In the crowd that night was the proverbial tall, dark, and handsome stranger. Born in Egypt to a Christian family from Lebanon, Nabil El Moussa had just begun his career as an electrical engineer. The two of them chatted, and before long, Nabil and Dominique were planning a life together.

At one point, my dad's work took him back to Beirut. The city was being torn apart by the Lebanese Civil War. Dad found himself, literally, in the crossfire. Because his apartment was on the top floor of a tall building, it would occasionally catch projectiles as they whizzed from east to west or north to south. One night, he telephoned my mom with a warning: "Don't come to Beirut! It's crazy!"

My mom doesn't listen to anyone, so she went anyway—and a week or two later, a rocket veered off target and exploded in their apartment. It blew up the whole kitchen, just ten feet or so from where the two of them were sitting. With that, my parents knew they had to leave. They fled the building and, as fast as they could, got themselves to the airport. Whatever they had, they left behind: car, bank account, everything. It was time to make a major change.

They made their way to Southern California. Mom went to work teaching French and Spanish at a high school. Dad began working for a company that supplied electronic controls to factories in the area. He quickly learned that some people had a problem with his name and his background. Snarky comments about camels and jockeys stunned him. Finally, he decided that to make a living and provide for his family, "Nabil" would have to become just "Bill." Then, for a last name, he borrowed the closest surname at hand: my mom's. Nabil El Moussa became "Bill Arnould." Meanwhile, my mom kept on being Dominique El Moussa. Yep: they flipped their names.

In 1986, we moved from Lakewood, California, to Buena Park, a gritty town just minutes from Disneyland and Knott's Berry Farm, but light-years away from the fantasies they were selling. We were now a family of four: Dominique and Bill; my seven-year-old sister, Angelique; and little Tarek, five. (My name, Tarek, sounds like "car wreck," but with a T instead of the C. Strangely appropriate, considering some of the situations I've been in. Tarek translates roughly as, "The one who knocks." I like that. I tend to be the one who knocks, over and over again.)

From our house in Buena Park, Mom quickly developed a reputation as "The Mom," not just to me and Angelique, but to all our friends. She was the mom all the kids loved. On weekends, our house became the place everybody wanted to go—and everyone was welcome. On a typical Saturday morning, while other parents were sleeping in, Mom would cook breakfast for everybody, then we'd pile into her big gray Dodge van and she'd drive us to the beach.

Buena Park was and is a melting pot. Among my Black and Hispanic friends growing up, I occasionally got teased for being *leche*—as pale as milk—but race didn't seem all that meaningful to us kids. The wealthiest kid I knew was Paul, one of my closest friends during those years, and still a friend today. Paul came from a Hispanic family that had made a dazzling success of their commercial painting company. Going to events or sports games with Paul's family, I often got picked up in a limo. On one memorable weekend, we stayed on the family's houseboat. From the deck, I could see their other boats, Jet Skis, and other toys that I started to dream about one day owning! That was when the seed was planted in my head that I wanted to be rich—I just didn't know how to get there.

Something my parents gave me, from the beginning, was an understanding of what it means to work, and work hard. Our mom may have been the "fun mom" throughout our childhood years, but she was also a workhorse. After teaching high school classes all day, she would tutor kids in the afternoon. When that was done, she'd come home and take care of us—cooking dinner, helping us with our homework, reading to us, and putting us to bed. Then she would fall into bed at who knows what hour. And whenever I wasn't in school, Mom was hauling me in the van to hockey practice or karate. Angelique and I were constantly going somewhere, and it was Mom who got us there. To sum up my memories of Mom during those years, I'll put it very simply: she worked her ass off.

As hard as it is for a teacher's kid to admit, school was never my favorite environment. It's not that I hated the work itself; in fact, I discovered early on that I had a gift for mental math. Math problems that other kids needed calculators for were puzzles that I enjoyed solving quickly in my head. What was agonizing for me was having to sit still in class, not being able to move, having to be quiet. You know: following the rules. Let's just say my attention deficit hyperactivity disorder (ADHD) made it difficult for me to learn the ABCs. My kindergarten teacher parked me at a desk in a back corner of the classroom, shielded behind a cardboard box that kept the other kids from seeing me. At five years old, I felt completely alone. I can still hear those buzzing fluorescent lights as I sat there behind that cardboard, desperate to be doing anything else.

Sports became the outlet for my pent-up energy. As soon as I turned eight, the second I got out of school, Dad would take me straight to the baseball field. He had me fielding ground balls, hitting, and practicing different pitches, over and over and over, for hours on end. This went on for years. And we weren't out there just enjoying some leisurely father-son time. Once I chose baseball, the understanding was that I was committed. Dad drove me hard. His expectations were high. With time, I outgrew Dad's coaching. I began going to the batting cages at Home Run Park in Anaheim, where I would hit balls for hours every day until my hands were blistered. Then, I would pitch. By the time I was in junior high, I was pitching fast and batting cleanup, and thinking seriously about a career in baseball.

When I recall those times on the baseball fields with my dad, what stands out for me is that he started out knowing absolutely nothing about the game. He was Middle Eastern and had spent some of his adolescent years in Europe. He had a lot of natural athletic ability, but for him, the only sport was soccer. Yet when he saw that I was interested in baseball, he recognized that "America's pastime" might be something I'd be good at. As soon as he saw that, this grown man with heavy responsibilities—and not all that much personal interest in baseball—forced himself to learn it.

As tough on me as my dad was—and no question, he was tough—he was always very supportive. Two or three days a week, he would show up at school to take me to lunch. Sometimes, he'd bring a sack of hamburgers for me and my friends. And throughout those years, his coaching never sounded like, "No, you can't do this." Instead, what my dad said, constantly, was, "Where you are today, Tarek, you can't. You can't do it now. But if you really want to do it, you can. You just have to practice, Tarek. *Practice.*"

Success proved him right. I began to learn that when you want something and you're willing to work for it, the dream becomes reality. The work of baseball became a joy. As I started my freshman year at Sunny

Hills High, I was pitching fast and throwing hard. I loved the leadership role that those two positions gave me. Whether I was standing on the mound or getting ready at the plate, all eyes were on me. I was under pressure to excel. And I discovered that I liked that pressure. I began to understand what people mean when they talk about being "in the zone." I became so absorbed in the challenge in front of me that I lost any sense of time. Soon, a career in the major leagues began to feel like a legitimate possibility. That's what I wanted, and I continued to work toward that goal.

Then, disaster struck. Just weeks into my freshman season, something went seriously wrong with the nerves in my right arm. Right after batting practice at Home Run Park, I headed over to the pitching section. It hurt to throw the ball, but I figured I was just rusty from the off-season. I tried to "pitch through" the pain. Big mistake. Before long, every pitch caused me to flinch in pain. That was a sign that I should have stopped. But I didn't. And that decision ruined my future in baseball. After I threw the very last pitch that night, my life was never the same. Soon enough, I began to see that I was probably done. I just couldn't play anymore. There was too much pain.

I stayed on the team over the next three years, suiting up, shagging balls, and hoping things would get better. But by senior year, I knew my dream had come to an end. I fell into a depression. I couldn't believe that baseball had been taken from me. I had just spent years of my life in what I thought were the beginning stages of a professional career. I felt outrageously cheated out of the activity I loved most—and out of the future I'd planned for myself.

Meanwhile, after years of keeping their marriage together for Angelique and me, our parents got divorced. The process started almost immediately after my high school graduation. So, having no idea who I was or what I really wanted in life, on the same day that I crossed the stage and got my diploma, I went home, gathered my things, and moved out. I was off to Newport Beach to start my new life in the triplex, with Ronnie.

Today, I'm twice the age that I was in that "hell year" of 2000–2001. I'd like to think I've learned some things since I was nineteen. Looking back, I could easily dismiss my teenage self as just a crazy, mixed-up kid, stumbling down a short detour on the way to maturity. But what I see now is how dangerously close I came to complete disaster. Not long ago, Paul, my old friend and classmate from houseboating days and beyond, shared with me something his dad had said about me years ago, when Paul and I were teenagers. "Your friend Tarek," he told Paul. "Let me tell you what I predict for Tarek: Tarek will end up either very, very rich—or very, very dead."

I've thought a lot about what Paul's dad saw, and about what I see now, with the perspective of twenty years. To begin with, I see someone who had lost his way. I dreamed of success, but I didn't know where to start. The excitement of baseball, of being The Man, was gone; I was depressed. The truth was, there was no compelling reason to get out of bed in the morning. I felt paralyzed by setbacks—my shoulder, my parents' divorce—that stole away my sense of purpose. And without that sense of purpose, I didn't know who I was. I was waiting for someone to tell me what to do, but that person wasn't stepping forward.

I needed to double-check my location.

DOUBLE-CHECKING YOUR LOCATION

Every project begins with understanding where you are, where you're starting from. Before you begin moving from "Here" to "There," you need an accurate idea of where "Here" is. In the flipping business, you want to understand the history of the house you're looking at. You need to drive around the neighborhood. You may need to make a few trips around the block to fully understand what you're seeing. For a doctor, this might mean taking a look at a patient's past medical records to understand their current condition. A lawyer listens carefully as the client talks about the events leading up to their decision to get legal help.

Getting an accurate take on your starting point can be hard. First impressions can be misleading. When you've lost your momentum and feel like you're stuck in a hole, I know how hard it can be to lift up your head and look around. But it's imperative that you take another look.

Double-checking your location means taking stock of your immediate resources. I wish someone had helped me reframe the experiences of my childhood years as tools, just waiting for me to put them to use. For starters, there were the life lessons I'd absorbed from my parents, the things that Angelique and I took for granted. They had made the bold decision to start life together in the middle of a civil war. When that became a life-or-death proposition, they dropped whatever wasn't essential, and they got the hell out of Beirut. They changed their negative circumstances in a hurry.

They also, without question, taught us about hard work. After putting down roots in a country foreign to both of them, they got busy doing whatever it took to help those roots flourish and grow strong. They worked their asses off and showed us that sometimes you do the thing you don't particularly like—for a while, anyway—in order to get closer to the thing you *do* like, later on. My parents showed us that as soon as something "catches fire"—as soon as what you're doing looks like it's working—you double down on it.

I wish I'd recognized these things as built-in assets to call on in order to get myself unstuck. Instead, the only voice I was listening to in Newport Beach was the contempt-filled voice inside my head. By the way, I don't think that nineteen-year-old Tarek was unique in his pessimistic, negative, self-sabotaging mindset. Other people, too, routinely cut themselves off from the steps that lead to happiness and success. They stumble around without a focus or a direction. When catastrophe comes, they're paralyzed. They wait for someone to tell them what to do and how to do it. They play those relentless tapes of self-pity and doubt in their heads. They give up, and they give up much too soon.

In my case, the solution that my nineteen-year-old self came up with was to drown my misery in alcohol. I drank and smoked and hated myself—then I drank and smoked some more. I kept abusing my mind and body. When Ronnie and I were finally, officially gone from the triplex, I changed addresses, but I didn't change my behaviors.

Finally, one night in December 2001, living in a borrowed house far from Newport, about to reach for the bottle of vodka, I heard myself say, "I've got to take a night off." Close to midnight, I stood up and went outside. I'll never forget that sensation of being outside, sober. I couldn't believe how wonderful everything smelled: the cut grass, the cool breeze—even the smell of the concrete porch seemed miraculous. With nothing in my body to blur my senses, it was as if I were having that experience—nighttime—for the first time in my life. And standing there outside, alone on the porch under the darkening December sky, I heard myself saying, "It's time for me to make some changes."

CHAPTER TWO

"FLIPPING 101"

I sometimes joke that if you want to follow my path to a "T," it's pretty simple. All you have to do is start by ruining your life, like I did. You look around and you think, *I've totally screwed this up, and I need to get going on building something better than the life I have now.* The truth is, I have completely rebuilt my life: who I am, what I am, what I believe in, and what I stand for, more than once.

In very simple terms, it all comes down to what I have done to create success in the world of real estate. The same fundamental rules that I've used to become "the world's best-known flipper" are rules that you, the reader, can and should use to turn your life around. They are rules that can help you have the success that you deserve.

This is what I do, once I've found a house that looks like it might be a promising flip:

- I evaluate the property. I take stock of its strengths and weaknesses, including any defects.

- I plan the rehab by looking closely at "comps": comparable sales of homes that have things in common with my project house.
- I renovate the property, I sell it, and I take my profit.
- *Then I do it all over again, but bigger and better.*

———

Like anyone else in business, I'm looking to buy low and sell high. If the target house is cheap enough, and I can find a way to turn it around and make a profit, I'm interested. I have to be confident that I'm buying the house at a discount to its future value. That means I use price comparisons from recent sales in that area to figure out what the house will probably sell for. As I look at the house, I get very analytical about the things I care about most: a solid roof, functional plumbing, and a sound foundation. I always want to know how motivated the owners are to sell, because that affects how fast I can close the deal, and at what price. Meanwhile, I keep an eye out for things about the house that I'm probably not going to be able to do anything about. Are those negative features deal breakers? Are there safety hazards or other defects in this house that will make it impossible for me to flip it at a profit? And, of course, I think about the timeline. Sometimes, it can feel as if there's nothing more expensive in the world than a house you've bought that is sitting there. You've poured your money into buying it and renovating it, and with every day that passes, that money is not working for you. So there is always a sense of urgency in what I do. The faster I finish the project, the faster I put that money back to work!

If everything works out, the day finally comes when I close on the sale and hand the keys to the new buyer. I celebrate, but not in the ways you might think. My version of celebrating involves going out in search of a new property to flip, or picking up the phone to call a broker about another opportunity. I like to call it "throwing gas on the fire." I love the momentum of starting the same process—the process that just netted me a nice profit—all over again.

So there, in a nutshell, is what I do. Allow me to make that process even simpler. Whether it's a house or your life we're talking about, what you need to do is follow these four steps:

- Evaluate
- Emulate
- Renovate
- Duplicate

ADAM

One of the first people I hired after I started flipping houses was a friend I had known since the summer before our freshman year of high school. Adam Lindholm and I met on the field for freshman football, and at first, we didn't get along. Adam and his friends had come up through the nicer, more "elite" elementary and junior high schools, and they already had their clique at Sunny Hills. My tiny group of Buena Park friends and I felt like intruders from the wrong part of town. So on the first day of practice, I walked over to where Adam and his friends were, and I helped myself to their water. I had decided to "plant my flag in the ground," so to speak. Plus, I was thirsty. Adam and his friends were stunned. Words were exchanged, and a couple of them threatened me. I responded, "Bring it on!" . . . and I'll just skip to the happy ending. Somehow, in spite of our rocky introduction, Adam and I became great friends.

Before long, Adam was spending a lot of weekends at my house. He wasn't an early riser, so on Saturday mornings, my mom would yell from the kitchen, "Adam! Wake up! Come get your *pancake*!" In Mom's French accent, it sounded more like "pen-kick." The promise of a delicious "pen-kick" never failed to get Adam out of bed. Soon his nickname was "Pancake."

No matter what kind of situation we found ourselves in, Adam was my reliable right-hand man in high school. He was soft-spoken and methodical, and I could count on him to stay calm in a crisis. And he wasn't afraid of work. By the time we graduated, Adam had already held a series of jobs: he had worked at a moving company, a video-rental store, a skateboard shop, and the appliance counter at Sears. He hadn't made much money, but he had always impressed his bosses and been promoted. After a short stint in college, he had gone directly into the working world.

Fast-forward about ten years. I was finally getting some traction in the flipping business, and things were going well enough that I knew I was ready to "scale up." I was managing all the construction for the flips. Meanwhile, leads were coming in on promising flip properties, and I needed to reach out to those potential sellers, fast. In addition, there was a lot of work to do coordinating the purchases I had already made. That meant getting the right signatures from the right people on the right documents. I couldn't possibly keep managing the construction, and knocking on doors, and calling all the leads, and handling all the closing paperwork by myself. I was overwhelmed, and I needed help.

By then Adam was living in the San Fernando Valley, north of Los Angeles. He worked for a window installation company not far from my real estate office. One night at a bar in downtown Fullerton, we started talking about real estate. I learned that Adam was commuting four or five hours, every day, to spend another eight hours installing windows—all for about $20,000 a year. I told him that, for a guy putting in thirteen-hour days, he was making pennies compared to what he could be making with me in real estate.

The "evaluation" stage—double-checking your location—is all about coming to grips with your own self-concept. It's about taking a hard look at the opinions and perceptions about yourself that you're carrying around with you. Until Adam and I had that conversation, he thought of himself strictly as a window installer. And as a window installer, he believed he was making the income that he deserved. It didn't take much reevaluation for Adam to see a different future for himself.

———

In the flipping world, good comps—price comparisons, from recently sold homes in the target neighborhood—help you understand the value of your project house. A comp is a preview of what the home might sell for once you fix it up. I've learned that comps are also a useful way of thinking about your life. Comps are your personal "what could be." Is your "current value" a fair and accurate understanding of what you're worth? Or have you undervalued yourself?

To answer these questions, I'm convinced that you need to look around for someone who's doing the kinds of things you'd like to do and living the kind of life you'd like to have. Find a person you'd like to be like, and who has done what you want to do, and then decide you're going to emulate them. Simply identifying a flesh-and-blood "comp" like this is a powerful step in a new direction.

All of us are works in progress, and when I reconnected with Adam, I wasn't even thirty years old. I was far from a "finished flip" myself. Experience comes from making a lot of mistakes, and I still had some to make! I still had a lot to learn. But what I could offer Adam, even then, was proof. I was living evidence of the kind of income he could make in real estate. Just as importantly, I could offer Adam some clear-cut steps for getting there. I knew enough about the "how-to" of flipping to be able to teach those things to Adam.

In other words, I was the comp that allowed Adam to rethink his situation. To emulate me, all he needed to do was jump. And fortunately for both of us, he jumped, immediately.

———

I was thrilled when Adam signed on. Eventually, he became a key member of my real estate team. But first there was hard work to do.

At this point, I'll share with you a nugget of real estate wisdom. A lot of success in real estate relies on doing what works, over and over again. You find strategies that work, and then you implement those strategies hour after hour, day after day. There are things I do in flipping that I take from one project house to the next; I don't reinvent what is already working. In flipping—as in life—you renovate. Once you figure out what works, be relentless about it. Take massive action, then do it again.

When Adam started working with me, here's the plan I gave him. Show up at the office at this time every morning; make this number of phone calls; go knock on this many doors; and don't come back until you've had at least fifty conversations with people who own houses. This is what you say. This is how you say it.

As with most things in life, the formula itself isn't hard. Doing the work in the formula is. Arnold Schwarzenegger could take someone who's five feet tall and weighs 300 pounds, and give them a fitness routine, a diet, and training supplements. But until that person puts Arnold's plan into action, they'll always be 300 pounds, right? It's not about "being willing" to do it. It's about doing it! And—in real estate, as in life—it's the "doing it" that matters. So as excited as I was to bring Adam on board, I made it clear to him that I could show him what to do, but I couldn't—and wouldn't—do it for him.

For the first couple of days, I took him out with me to knock on doors. It was the middle of the summer, and we drove all over the Inland Empire, the sprawling suburbs east of Los Angeles. We talked about the fact that life is a contact sport, and when you want something, you have to make contacts: you have to talk to people. When you knock on one door, that person may not be planning to sell their house. When you knock on thousands of doors and talk to hundreds of people, eventually you'll find someone who wants to sell.

After two days of these "ride-alongs" with me, Adam was on his own. I set him loose. And Adam proved that he was more than willing. He showed me he would do it.

Every morning, after making his phone calls, he would get in his car and drive east. At night he'd come back and tell me what had happened that day. Even when you've been doing it for years, the work can be awful and frustrating. The days were long, and hot, and filled with rejection. But Adam was relentless. He didn't quit. Day after day, he showed up. He kept going. And that's what it takes. The moment you decide to make changes in your life—to renovate—you've got to become relentless about it.

———————

Once Adam proved to me that he was willing to knock on doors for listings, I decided to bring him into the investment world. In real estate, and especially flipping, the early bird gets the worm. You've got to stay ahead of your competition. In flipping, it starts with finding "distressed" properties. These are homes with loans in default, homes in probate, and homes identified as "short sales," meaning they're priced to sell for less than the owners owe. My thinking was, while our competitors were still drinking their morning coffee, we could be hustling. We could be looking for any distressed properties on the market and putting together offers on them.

So I gave Adam a new mission. Every morning at 7:30, he was to get on his computer, pull up MLS—the local multiple listing service database—and find all the new listings that had hit the market since the night before. We knew that if we were the first ones to make contact with the agent, it increased our odds of getting the deal. For every distressed sale listed, I told Adam to call the listing agent. If the agent didn't respond,

Adam was to leave a voicemail, explaining what we wanted. Then, the second he hung up, he was to send that same agent a text message. Finally, he was to copy and paste the agent's email address, then send an email with the same question he had just left in the voicemail and the text message.

The name I gave this system was "MLS domination," and I told Adam that for MLS domination to work, he needed to be fast. I challenged him to go from voicemail to text message to email all within thirty seconds. There was nothing magical about the process itself. It was all about duplication. Do this; then do it again; then go to the next distressed listing and do it again, over and over.

Soon we had our system up and running. "Team Tarek" was operating at full speed, with Adam in a central role. We turned MLS domination into a recipe for success, and Adam used that recipe, day in and day out, to close deals and make money. About a year after he started, Adam was making a six-figure income. Before long, in a typical month, he earned multiples of what he'd made in a year of installing windows. Eventually, I asked Adam to become president of the entire flipping business, Tarek Buys Houses, and he agreed. He had bought into the basic steps—evaluate, emulate, renovate, and duplicate—and he was seeing the results.

CHAPTER THREE

EVALUATE

EARLY ARRIVAL

My arrival into this world was less than smooth. Eight months into her pregnancy, my mom developed such terrible pain that she had to be hospitalized. Looking back, my mom thinks this medical crisis was caused by some antibody she picked up in a blood transfusion she got as a teenager. But back then, the doctors were telling her, "Your baby is struggling. We don't know whether he'll survive. We can do a C-section now, but his lungs are not developed enough for him to breathe on his own." And then they gave her a choice. "We can give you an experimental drug, to jump-start the baby's lungs. But if things go wrong, which one do you want us to save: you, or the baby?"

Thankfully, my mom's decision—the baby—never had to be acted on. I was taken out by C-section, weighing barely five pounds, and rushed to the neonatal intensive care unit. That's where I spent the first ten days of my life, scrawny, yellow, and intubated, under a warming lamp. During those ten days, I had five blood transfusions. But apparently, I was not out of the woods. At one point, a hospital staffer—some tech my mom had never seen before—strolled into her room and announced, completely out of the blue, "You need to be prepared. We think your son may have cerebral palsy."

My parents were terrified. I can't help thinking about how different this baby boy was from the son that my dad had probably imagined. In the world Bill grew up in—Egypt in the 1960s—everyone's male hero was a dashing film actor named Omar Sharif. Like my dad and his boyhood friends, Omar Sharif was a Lebanese Christian born in Egypt. He had broken free of his humble beginnings in a major way. By the mid-1960s, Sharif had been nominated for an Academy Award and was an international superstar. Tall, athletic, and brilliant, he spoke five languages and was ranked as one of the top fifty bridge players in the world. For young Egyptian men like my dad, Omar Sharif had it all. He was the ultimate symbol of what an "outsider"—an immigrant kid from an ethnic minority—could become.

And then there was the reality of me, in those early days: I was frail and jaundiced, and I began to show signs of some kind of palsy. As I got older, I developed weird tics. Without warning, completely at random, my head would shake violently from side to side. Many times, this shaking was accompanied by a loud, involuntary snort. And whenever I was sitting, one of my knees would bounce. My strange behaviors startled other kids, and they would laugh. I got picked on a lot—even by adults who should have known better. One of our coaches liked to ask me, in front of the whole team, "Hey, Tarek, do you want a million bucks?" And when my head shook—involuntarily, of course—he'd say, "You *don't*?" Then he'd enjoy the laughter he created.

Naturally, I was unhappy about all the twitching and snorting and bouncing. But I did my best to get out in front of the problem. At home, when one of my violent head shakes came on, I'd say, "Look, Dad! I can bite my own ear!"

It's an approach I've tried to take throughout my life. Even if I can't always make things funny, I do everything I can to find something positive in a negative situation. I try to find the opportunity in it. I remind myself to evaluate things the right way.

"DISTRESSED" IS A GOOD PLACE TO START

Picture overgrown grass and piles of garbage in the front yard of a home. When you evaluate it one way, that property is just an eyesore; it's something ugly. But evaluate it a different way, and that ugliness may spell opportunity. To a house flipper, the uncut grass and the piles of garbage may be good signs. They may point to a future "win-win": a happy outcome for both the homeowner and the flipper.

Typically, the owner of a distressed property is struggling. They're overwhelmed by emotional and financial distress. Now suppose that the overgrown grass and the garbage catch the eye of an investor, and the investor knocks on the door and starts a conversation with the homeowner. During that conversation, the homeowner reveals that they're anxious and feeling stuck. The investor learns the homeowner is highly motivated to put the mess behind them and move on. If the two parties can come to an agreement, and that house changes hands, then both of them win. The homeowner gets some financial and emotional relief, and the investor gets a chance to clean things up and make some profit.

This is a "flipping fundamental." To be a successful real estate investor, you must train yourself to evaluate every property in the right way. You must look at the property not just as it is now, but as it might be. The

ugliest, most awful house on the street is often the one that, once it's renovated, throws the other houses into the shade.

I don't know what your particular source of distress is right now. I
do know that "distressed" can mean opportunity. It can be what motivates you to take the first steps in the right direction and to put a messy
past behind you. Just like that ugly house, everybody has the potential
to improve. You have to believe that every problem and every product
and every property has the potential for improvement. Every "flop" can
become a flip. I know that because I've lived it.

For years, my severe ADHD was a major source of distress. It made
school a miserable experience for me. When you have attention problems,
it can feel as if you are constantly waiting for something to happen. You
wait and you wait...and nothing happens. I couldn't keep still. One day,
my sixth-grade teacher got so frustrated with my hyperactivity that he
slammed me against the wall. That made two of us who were unhappy
with me! In that environment, in those conditions, I was in terrible
distress—just like the houses I buy.

Here's the flip side. I'm convinced that my ADHD has been a key
element in my success. Once I learned to challenge myself to think cre-
atively and tackle new goals, my ADHD no longer felt like torture. I
couldn't make it go away, but I could acknowledge it, and I could get
ahead of it.

At a critical point in my real estate career, I set myself a goal of making fifty contacts a day on the telephone. To get that number of conversations, I learned I had to make about five hundred phone calls a day. This
wasn't a robocaller or an auto-dial machine. It was just me, in a cubicle,
with my phone and a list of numbers. And to keep myself accountable, to
make sure I hit my daily goal, I made a game out of those phone calls. I
made the game very physical. I would try to see how fast I could dial the
number; then I'd let it ring exactly three times; then, if no one answered, I

would immediately hang up and dial the next number. Each time, I tried to dial even faster. It was all about finger dexterity and speed. Making a game of this process forced me to stay intensely focused. I was able to "outrun" my ADHD, if that makes sense. And many, many of those calls turned into successful sales.

All of this may help to explain why I love flipping houses. The work is intense, quick, and full of action. There's no time to get bored when things are moving in a hundred different directions. There's a lot to do, and I get results, fast.

A Persian friend once paid me this interesting compliment. He told me there's a Persian proverb that goes, "No one can carry five melons at the same time; you're lucky if you can carry two." And then he said, "But you, Tarek—you carry at least five melons, all the time!" I know exactly what he means. I'm one of those people who work best with the TV on, music playing in the background, and four or five "top priority" projects on my desk. Because I know I get bored easily, I'm intentional about working on a bunch of different things at the same time. For me, carrying five melons—or more!—keeps me interested and engaged.

In other words, I've learned to use my "distress" as a source of energy. Other people might look at all my multitasking and call it chaos. But I happen to know that my so-called chaos makes me productive. Multitasking is how I've learned to "flip" my ADHD. A short attention span might seem like a liability, but I know it can be an asset. It's all about how you evaluate your situation.

THE APPRAISAL

Let's face it: the idea of honestly evaluating yourself can be terrifying. It means asking difficult questions, such as *Who am I?* and *Am I where I want to be in life?* Those kinds of questions can make you so uncomfortable that you avoid asking them. After all, who wants to ask a question when they know they may not like the answer?

I recognize that "self-appraisal" can be very difficult. Most adults, let alone kids, would have a hard time telling you honestly what's going on inside them. It can be very hard to evaluate ourselves. I get that.

So—the flipper that I am—let me approach it with you this way. A lot of flippers out there will take the crappiest house you can imagine, and they'll put "lipstick on a pig": they paint it, they put in new grass, and they sell it—but they disregard the inside, what's behind the walls. The house might need new plumbing, new wiring, new drywall, whatever. Some of those things may pose real danger. But those flippers are counting on the buyer to overlook that stuff. From the outside, the house looks great. But, of course, on the inside, the house is in shambles. The defects and the hazards have been covered up. When the poor buyers move into that house, they're screwed. Sadly, I see this kind of thing all the time.

The fact is that you've got to look at what's deep inside the house, behind the drywall, if you want the house to shine. You go inside, and you look at what's there. If it needs new plumbing, new electric, new drywall—whatever it might be—you take care of those things. When you ignore those interior things, there are consequences.

Just as in flipping, you have to perform this kind of appraisal on yourself. It can be hard, but you have to do it. And just as in flipping, it helps to have an appraisal checklist: a scorecard of what you're looking for. You want to make sure you're evaluating your "inside" in the right way.

The Healthy Self

When your "inside" is healthy:

- You know who you are and what you stand for.
- You respect yourself.

- You know what you want and what you need.
- You're okay with expressing your emotions. You recognize that your emotions are an essential part of who you are, and you know how to demonstrate them in an appropriate way.
- You recognize your need to have other people in your life, and you're able to connect with those other people in ways that are good for them and good for you.
- Sure, life throws challenges at you from time to time. But as those challenges come, you're confident that you have what it takes to manage them.
- You have a feeling of momentum: your overall experience is of making progress toward your goals. Notice I said *your goals*, not someone else's goals for you.

The Unhealthy Self

As you'll learn, at various points in my life I have flunked one or more of the items on the healthy self scorecard. I've batted a thousand on the unhealthy self instead. Thankfully, I understand the difference.

Think of the unhealthy self as a bundle of bad assumptions. It's a set of incorrect beliefs about "the way things are" and the way they're "supposed to be." These mistaken assumptions affect how you engage with the world. See which of the following statements apply to you:

- The unhealthy self assumes that "everyone is happy except me." When you're hurting, it's so easy to think that no one else is. But the truth is—as the actor Michael J. Fox once put it—"We all get our own bag of hammers." Everybody is carrying around something heavy, something they're struggling with. I myself have dealt with multiple mental health issues, including depression. My first marriage exploded in living color all over the tabloids and media outlets. I've had multiple cancers. And I'm not the only one who has fallen into that trap of thinking, *No one else could possibly feel what I'm feeling right now.*

- The unhealthy self lives according to someone else's expectations. It's as if someone else has designed the home that you're supposed to live in for the rest of your life, but it's a crappy home! Not good.

- The unhealthy self is obsessed with how other people see them. It's natural to see ourselves as other people see us. But it can become an obsession, a nonstop source of anxiety and self-hatred.

- The unhealthy self says, *I was just born this way, and that's all there is to it.* It says, I am what I am because of biology. It's all in my genes, and there's nothing I can do about it. (For a while, that's how I thought about my own ADHD.)

- Another unhealthy self-concept is the belief that my life is the way it is because of some external force, some setback that has permanently disrupted my life. "I'm a victim of the pandemic." "My business partners screwed me over, and I'll never recover." I've had close friends who got caught up in this kind of thinking. I've had to tell them, "That ship has sailed. That's ancient history! *It's time to move on.*"

- Here's another version of the unhealthy self, one I'm seeing more and more of these days. Call it "false self-esteem." People with false self-esteem are puffed up with the mistaken idea that they're special in some way. Their whole lives, they've been told that they're a (fill in the blank: musical genius; tennis prodigy; academic superstar). They expect to get a medal or a trophy just for showing up! Then, when the first setback happens—the first time they realize that they're not superior—their unhealthy self-concept gets crushed! The experience is so unfamiliar, and so painful, that they're paralyzed. They think, *This can't be happening!*

- There's also the self that wants to "overshare." This one says, *I have a million different feelings. All of my feelings are very important to the other people in my life. Whenever I display my feelings, then the other people in my life are supposed to take care of me and my many feelings.* This is completely wrong. There's no question that being able to communicate how you feel is essential to your well-being. But when you start talking about your feelings for the hundredth time, and you notice that the people around you already look exhausted, that's a clue. It's a clue that it's time to take action and fix your problems!

OWNING IT

Back when I played baseball, I loved hitting a line drive. There was nothing better than connecting with the ball and bringing runners home. I especially loved how it felt—easy, no strain, like the most natural thing in the world. That's how it feels when you find the sweet spot on the bat and drive the ball. That's also how it feels when your self-concept is healthy and you're making progress toward your dreams.

And that kind of health is your right. You have a right to experience that "sweet spot" on a regular basis.

But with that right comes responsibility. There's work involved, and you can't expect to put all that work on someone else. If your self-concept is messed up, it's on you to take the actions necessary to change it. Sure, other people can help. All of us need trusted friends, people we can rely on for wise counsel. But at the end of the day, this is your "flip," your project—no one else's! When it comes to a fully developed, healthy self-concept, no one is just going to give it to you. You need to work for it!

Think of this as the foundation that everything else is built on. Having a healthy foundation is about committing yourself to creating the life you want instead of passively accepting whatever comes your way. It's about knowing who you are, recognizing your worth, and taking ownership of your outcomes.

Listen to some things people tell themselves that indicate serious problems with their foundations. Do any of these sound familiar?

- "I am where I am right now as a result of bad luck."
- "My lot in life is a product of chance."
- "It's my destiny to be where I am."
- "It's my boss's/spouse's/parents' fault."
- "I don't have the talent for it."
- "I'm not smart enough."
- "I'm a Sagittarius. It's just the way we are."

Are you seeing the theme here? In every one of these explanations, people want to make the causes of their problems external. But this kind of thinking will only hold you back. Just like cracks in the foundation of a home, it's a defect that will affect every other part of your project. And until you fix the foundation, your project is in jeopardy.

People who operate from a solid foundation think differently. After years of studying successful people, I've learned how they think. They tend to think and say things like:

- "What happens to me is my own doing."
- "If I'm smart about it and take care of myself, I can stay healthy."
- "Becoming a success is a matter of hard work."
- "When I make plans, I am almost certain I can make them work."
- "Getting what I want has little or nothing to do with luck."

- "In the long run, the respect that people get in this world is the respect they deserve."
- "I create my own results in this world; no one is going to do it for me."

"Strong foundation" thinkers are people who engage the world with the attitudes in the second list. These people tend to be happier at work, enjoy better health, and have more influence in the world than people who blame external forces for their problems. They are less likely to quit their jobs, and they're more likely to get promoted. Put simply, they perform at a higher level and are more likely to be rewarded.

Here's just one example of how this principle can play out. More than once, someone has approached me on the street and said, "Hey, Tarek! I want to flip houses with you!" And that's it. I have no idea what they expect me to say. Compare that to someone who comes up to me and says, "Hey, Tarek, I want to flip houses with you, and I've been studying the market for three years. I've done a price analysis on fifty houses, and I've connected with sixteen different contractors. I know the price per foot to build in the city." To that person I say, "*Let's talk.*" The first person has a want; the second person has a want and a willingness to do the work. That second person is already taking ownership of their outcomes. That's what I call a strong foundation.

DIGGING DEEPER

Earlier I said that you have to deal with the inside of a house: you go inside, and you look at what's there. The first time I walk through a house I want to flip, I must get a read on what needs changing (obviously). But, just as importantly, I'm taking stock of things that I'm just not going to be able to change.

If you watch my shows, you know that I'm all about demo and the upgrade: rip that shelving out, replace that kitchen counter, enlarge that closet. Nevertheless, once in a while my crew and I come up against things we just can't change. Maybe the next-door neighbor is an obnoxious dude with a three-legged pit bull that howls all night. I can't change that. Maybe the house sits right under the flight path to LAX airport. I can't change that, either. We learn about the bad neighbor, or being under a flight path, and we look at each other and say, *Too bad*. Nothing we can do.

My point is, certain things "just are the way they are." There are some things that I just can't fix, no matter how much I want to. It's one of the hardest lessons that I've had to learn, both in business and in life. As a kid, I couldn't make my tics go away; I couldn't stop my head from shaking, or my knee from bouncing. Later on, much more serious things happened in my life, and I couldn't stop those, either.

But here's the important lesson. On my TV shows, those occasional setbacks are totally outnumbered by things that can be changed. The number of "nonnegotiable" things is much smaller than the number of things we *can* change. It's the same with life. Very few things in your life "just are." The list of things we can't change about ourselves is a very short list—much shorter than the list of things we can change.

This, too, calls for some honest evaluation. You need to ask yourself, What is it about me that's "permanent"? What are the things about me that I can't really change, even if I wanted to? When you really take the time to think about them, the list is pretty damn short!

Okay, you inherited certain physical characteristics from your parents. Your eye color, your height, literally everything about you, physically—those things were "programmed" into you at birth. You came into the world with them. Then, as you grew up, you were affected by the environment and by the way you were raised. As time passed, you probably believed whatever the people around you told you about who you were. Your understanding of your "self" was based almost entirely on the messages you got from other people. Your answer to *Who am I?* was, basically, *I am whoever those people say that I am.*

This may have been especially true when you were a teenager. As teenagers, all of us tend to obsess over what other kids think about us. Hopefully, as you got older, you started to play a much larger role in developing your own identity. Hopefully, you pushed back against the identity that other people had been creating for you, and you started to create one on your own. That's what a lot of adolescent rebellion is about.

That's the way it's supposed to work, anyway. We're supposed to get to the point where we are comfortable in our own skin. We're supposed to take ownership of who we are and what we stand for. We're supposed to take control of our own lives.

But often—very often—people get stuck.

A lot of people are way too easily convinced that huge parts of their lives are nonnegotiable. Much too quickly—and often permanently—they decide that the challenges or difficulties in their lives "just are," and there's nothing they can do about it. And as soon as they convince themselves of that, they give up on all kinds of opportunities. They quit looking for opportunities to find out what they're capable of.

Sometimes, they blame it on biology: "I'm a victim of my genes, and there's nothing I can do about it." The truth is, that's just a cop-out: it's an excuse you tell yourself that prevents you from accomplishing your goals. Sometimes, people keep playing the messages they've heard about themselves from other people, whether they're true or not. Or they listen to their own inaccurate and untruthful messages about who they are. And the sad part is, they continue living as if these assumptions—or lies!—about themselves are truths. They "overcount" the things they think are permanent and unchangeable.

THE FLIP SIDE

Let's recap. I sincerely believe that every problem has the potential to be flipped. Looking back, I see that a lot of the most miserable moments in my life could have been avoided if I had just "gone inside" and worked on my inner self—if I had just dug deeper.

When you honestly look at the bones of a house, and you see things that need to be fixed, you take care of those things. Of course, there are going to be challenges. But you accept responsibility for addressing those challenges as well as you can. Often, that means finding a way to turn your "defects" into strengths. You don't pretend they're not there. You don't throw drywall over an exposed wire and pretend there's no problem. Instead, you look for a safe plan to deal with the issue. You acknowledge your ADHD, or whatever it is you have, and you figure out how to make it work for you. You refuse to be limited by what you can't change.

Here's an interesting one: fear. My biggest fear in life has always been the fear of failure. But I try to make my fear work for me. I flip it this way: I've learned to tell myself, *You only fail if you quit.*

Imagine setting yourself a goal of losing twenty pounds in twenty days. When the twenty days are up, and you haven't lost all twenty pounds, do you quit? Have you failed? You only fail if you give up on your ultimate goal, which is to lose the twenty pounds! So when I fail, I keep going. I don't quit. I fail all the time, but I'll never quit, which means I'll never be a failure.

In other words, I use that unpleasant feeling—fear—to keep me moving, to keep me on the hunt for opportunity. I don't let an experience of failure tell me who I am. The point is that even though you can't rewire some basic things about yourself, you can find a way to declare a truce with them. You have to stop taking them so damn seriously all the time. Most importantly, you've got to redirect them in a positive way.

DIRTY MIRRORS

No chapter on evaluating yourself would be complete if I didn't acknowledge a special situation. I've already said that self-appraisal can be very difficult, and that's especially true when your perceptions are clouded by negative self-talk.

When it comes to negative self-talk, and the massive problems it creates, I speak from experience. Some of my biggest and most painful battles have taken place inside my head. In life, just like a house flip, there is a certain amount of demolition involved. Expectations change. Plans crumble. Things you thought were surefire wins end in failure. And sometimes, when you find yourself in those situations, it can be hard to see yourself clearly. It's like looking at yourself in a dirty mirror.

Just about every task in renovating a house—pulling up an old floor, remodeling a kitchen, scraping popcorn off a ceiling—causes all kinds of stuff to get kicked into the air. Those dust clouds always seem to find the closest mirror. It's as if the mirrored glass attracts the dust before anything else. It makes for some strange, sometimes disturbing reflections. When you look at yourself, it's not an accurate reflection of who you are.

At times I've struggled with dark thoughts, messages about myself that seemed powerful and real. That's the reality of depression. I know what it's like to be knocked down by life and then feel paralyzed. Setbacks and failures are often followed by negative self-talk. Afterward, I look back and realize that I've been looking in a dirty mirror.

Here are some important things I've learned. I've learned that *how you think determines how you feel*. How you feel, emotionally, is a result of the thoughts you're having. That means you have to pay attention to what you're telling yourself! Just like a filthy mirror, negative self-talk distorts your reality. It alters the facts, often in a convincing way. In the midst of the crisis, you start telling yourself things like this:

- "It's all my fault." Negative self-talk always wants to make the bad situation personal to you.
- "Everything I do turns out badly." Whatever the situation, negative self-talk makes it feel like your entire life is a mess. It makes you feel that the badness has infected every area of your life.

Two of its favorite words are *always* and *never*. Negative self-talk makes the situation feel permanent.

As difficult as it might be, when you start hearing negative self-talk, you have to argue with it. By "arguing," I mean *you have to get as skeptical with your own self-talk as you would be with any con artist.* You have to be willing to call BS on your self-talk, and you have to confront it with reason. You have to ask questions. Is the difficult situation you're in really your fault? Will the situation just go on and on forever? *Really?* And does everything you do turn out for the worst? Everything? *Really?*

By the way, these are just the kinds of questions a counselor or a wise friend would be asking if they were sitting there with you. I'll be the first to say that professional help can be extremely valuable, and wise friends are priceless. I also know that, sometimes, you've got to do this work on your own. So ask yourself, What would that counselor or friend have to say about all my negative thinking? Wouldn't they be calling BS on it?

This is the fight of your life! You have to keep chasing your dreams. You can't let that little voice win. You have to fight it like you've never fought before. You have to commit to this fight, and you have to take massive action.

Which brings me to another thing I've learned about dealing with negative thoughts. *Get up and do something.* Massive action requires... action! You need to take a step in a positive direction. And here I'm talking about a physical action, even something as simple as gathering up the trash and tossing it out; walking around the block; or spending thirty minutes at the gym. Instead of sitting there with your thoughts, commit to doing a physical task for a certain number of minutes, just to start with. See how far you get. Break that task up into manageable pieces. Set yourself a timer, if you want, but *go do something.*

In other words, call BS on your mixed-up thinking, and then get up and start moving. Find something you can actually do that will give you a sense of satisfaction and hope—even just a little. Look for the next little win, and go do it!

I'm here to tell you, those little wins add up. I know from experience that once you start with a little win, it propels you to a bigger one, and then a bigger one after that. With every little win, you gain some confidence. So go for the little win, and see what happens!

CHAPTER FOUR

EMULATE

AFTER-REPAIRED VALUE

Over the years I've flipped some of the nastiest houses you can imagine—the kinds of houses you'll never set foot in during your lifetime. I'm talking beyond your run-of-the-mill disgusting smells. I can't count the number of times I've walked into a property and thought, "Meth house." I've seen glass pipes, scorched spoons, and burn marks in the lawn where the meth cooks have dumped their chemicals. Mysteriously, one house even had knives stuck in the walls. Early in my career, my crew and I were taking a first look at a project house, and overhead I spotted a suspicious-looking brown stain on a ceiling tile. I grabbed a stepladder and climbed up to take a look. The instant I poked at that tile, cockroaches started pouring from the ceiling. There were thousands of them, skittering all over my head, down my legs, between my feet, and up the walls.

But remember: "distressed" means opportunity. In flipping, if you let yourself get distracted by the smells, the filth, the clutter, the traces of meth, the knives, or the cockroaches, then you'll never start. Beginning investors encounter those things, and they walk away. You can't do that. No matter how disturbing those things might be, you have to keep your focus on the future. You have to look ahead to the day when the renovation is finished, all of your costs have been accounted for, and the project house is sparkling clean and smells brand new.

Whenever I focus on that moment, I'm asking myself, *How much can you sell this house for?* That dollar amount—the house's "after-repaired value," or ARV—is the end result, the target I'm aiming for. The ARV is what I'm hoping to sell the house for after it has been repaired. It's what keeps me motivated. The ARV helps me stay on track over the days and weeks of renovation that are coming. In other words, by shifting my thinking from the "what is" to the "what can be," I'm building up momentum. I'm not blind to the "what is." But I don't stay there. That mental shift—to the "what can be"—is sometimes difficult. But it's essential.

So, yes, as the cockroaches cascaded down my body, you can bet I was cussing. So were the guys on my crew. One guy actually dashed outside so he could throw up. But by the time he finished and came back inside, I had already figured out how much money I was going to make on that house. I knew how much I had bought it for, and I had a very clear picture of sales prices in the neighborhood. The ARV looked great. And sure enough, the price I sold that house for turned out to be plenty. My profit made dealing with all of that nastiness worth it.

LOOK AT YOUR COMPS

Let's dig a little deeper into this question of value. How, exactly, does a flipper determine the ARV of a project house? The seller has listed a price that may or may not reflect what the house is really worth. Meanwhile, you hope to sell the renovated property for a number that makes you a handsome profit. But how do you figure out what either of those numbers should be?

The short answer is: by making comparisons. Maybe you look at real estate websites where similar homes are offered for sale. You study online databases, such as a broker's listing service or the county tax assessor's records. You pay careful attention to recently sold properties: comparable sales that have things in common with the house you hope to buy and renovate. You have to make sure you're comparing apples to apples.

I've learned to do these kinds of things—to find out all I can about the house—before I even go there. I need to know that spending the time and effort of going to the house will be worth it. Then and only then do I go there. I drive around. I scope out the neighborhood where the project house is located, and I try to get a sense of what neighboring properties are worth. I stop at "For Sale" signs. I grab sales flyers. My analysis goes like this: Here's the house I'm thinking about buying, in "as is" condition; over there is the comp house. I work out how much I'll have to spend to make my project house look as nice as the comp house that gave me my ARV. That tells me how much to offer for the house. I may make an offer without actually seeing the house, but I don't make an offer without doing comparisons.

Comps are vital information. It's no exaggeration to say that real estate prices are largely driven by them. For anyone in real estate, evaluating comps is an essential skill. It takes time to develop, but there's no substitute for it. A good comp is one that gives you a reasonable understanding of where your numbers might land. Ideally, the numbers look great, and your comps spark excitement about the profit you can expect once you've finished all the renovation work.

In other words, *a comp is a bridge between what is and what may be.* It's a real-life example of what your house could be.

A good comp brings the future into the present in a realistic and understandable way. It allows you to think about your project house as it is now, while at the same time giving you a reasonable idea of what it might become. It gives you a concrete picture of what you can achieve. A bad comp tells you . . . well, almost nothing. In very simple terms, the information you get from a bad comp is information you can't use, because it simply doesn't match up with your project.

Whenever I pull up a comp on my computer screen, and I start looking at the listing photos and the square footage and the price of that comp, I'm definitely thinking about the numbers. I'm also thinking about the people behind that listing: the seller, of course, but also the broker and the agent and even the contractors and subs who have "packaged" that house and are presenting it for sale. I'm not saying I actually know who they are in every case; I almost never do. But I do know that flesh-and-blood people are involved. And here's what I always tell myself: *They're doing it, so I know it can be done.*

———

Speaking for myself, my "ARV," my personal vision of the good life, has always involved financial success. And even as a kid, I saw business as the way to get there. I can't say I knew a lot of successful businesspeople when I was growing up, but early on I figured out there was a connection between success in business and having what I saw as "the good life." People like Paul's dad, and the other businesspeople I knew about, triggered my curiosity. They fired my imagination with dreams of what I might become. People like that became my "comps." They had done it, so I knew it could be done. I understood, almost instinctively, that it would take work. But I knew in my bones that I wasn't afraid of hard work. If the work involved a little bit of show business, so much the better!

My first big venture was a T-shirt company that my classmate Jenna and I started when we were fifteen. We designed cool art that we then put on T-shirts, with hopes of selling them wherever we could. I even went down to the courthouse to secure our company name. But because I was young and naïve, I made mistakes, and I didn't file the paperwork properly. After Jenna and I had spent our life savings printing five hundred T-shirts, a company with the identical name—which had filed the paperwork properly!—started making clothing. And that shut us down. We hadn't even sold a single T-shirt! To this day, I'm pretty sure those boxes of T-shirts are still in my mom's garage.

Later in high school, Ronnie and I found ourselves working at a pizza joint, making and delivering pizzas. One day we started tossing the dough back and forth to each other. We heard laughter, and we noticed that the customers were enjoying our little show. So Ronnie and I upgraded it. We began squaring off on opposite sides of the kitchen, as far apart as possible, and flinging the spinning dough all the way across the kitchen. We repeated that performance every night, and people loved it. A little bit of razzle-dazzle turned out to be great for business.

I took the money I made from the pizza job and, with my dad's help, invested it in the stock market. That was my first experience of being an investor. When the time was right—I had just turned eighteen—I cashed out and bought myself a motorcycle, a black and yellow Suzuki superbike. I did this without my parents' permission, and when I came home with that bike, it didn't go over well. Everyone was sure I was going to die.

Shortly after that, I took a job as a server at a Medieval Times restaurant. My work uniform consisted of a beige V-neck blouse, a kilt made out of brown pleather, and beige tights. My job was to carry fully loaded trays from the kitchen to the "lords and ladies" seated in rows of benches, offering them "Chicken. Chicken. Chicken." Then I'd come back around with another tray: "Bread. Bread. Bread." The work itself was repetitive, but I liked the physicality of it—and the showbiz element. Early on, I recognized that my real job there was to keep my customers entertained. And

I especially enjoyed the tips I made, which often came to $120 or $130 in a single night. That was big money when minimum wage was $5.75 an hour.

Shortly after that, I started another entrepreneurial venture—similar to the T-shirts, but much more sophisticated. I started a craft beer company. My plan was to show up at parties with beer that I had brewed and bottled myself, and sell it for $2 a bottle. There were three flaws in my plan. The first flaw was that I was underage. The second was that the beer tasted like chalk. And the third was that—terrible taste or not—my buddies and I drank up all the profits!

———

Is the "current value" you put on yourself a fair and accurate understanding of what you're worth? Or have you undervalued yourself?

In order to answer those questions, I'm convinced that you need a comp—or two, or three!—meaning flesh-and-blood sources of both inspiration and direction. You need people whose own success stories can guide and fuel your journey.

Throughout my life, I've encountered people whose success was so exciting to me that I couldn't wait to create a version of it for myself. I studied those people carefully to figure out how they did it, and to learn what I could do to emulate them and improve upon their achievements. I've used them to evaluate how I'm doing. To put this another way, if you're not actively chasing a comp—if you're not doing everything you can to emulate somebody whose success excites you—then you're missing out on a major opportunity.

Maybe you object to all of this because you think I'm telling you, on the one hand, to "be yourself," and on the other hand to find someone to copy. If so, we need to get clear on some things.

You can't help measuring yourself against others. Consciously or not, you're doing something like this all the time with the people you meet. You hear about someone who's dealing with a major challenge, and you think, *Gosh, I thought things were bad for me right now; I had no idea how lucky I was.* At other times, we do the comparison, and it's not in our favor. We measure our job status, our talents, titles, or material possessions—even our kids!—against what other people have, and—rationally or not—we decide that we come up short.

Sadly, because we now live in an age of constant social media, this behavior has become more intense than ever. We are bombarded with images and posts of people who may or may not be worthy of our attention. Yet it's so easy to play that comparison game, even when we know that the game is rigged against us. We compare ourselves to people on social media and decide, again, that we fall short.

The good news is that it's possible to play this game in a way that is healthy and uplifting. It's healthy when you find yourself thinking, *That person is successful; that's exciting. I want to be successful, too.* Unlike the kind of envy that makes you want to pull the other person down to a lower level, this "healthy envy" makes you want to pull yourself up to theirs.

The point is that, one way or another, you're going to choose comps. Consciously or not, you're going to allow certain people out there to influence your own behaviors. What I'm saying is, *Do this with intention.* Insist that their influence be a positive influence. What counts as positive influence? The answer is pretty simple. Positive influence is whatever serves to motivate, inspire, inform, and strengthen your own vision of where you want your life to be.

This practice has seen me through some dark times. Whenever setbacks come, or plans fail, I know that one of the fastest ways for me to "course correct" is to focus on a comp. I use their success story as the fuel I need to excite me and get me moving in the right direction again. There's just no substitute for the energy boost you get from looking at someone successful and reminding yourself, *They're doing it, so I know it can be done.*

By that awful year of 2001, I had no comps, and I had no direction. I was driving a black Toyota truck—my pride and joy—from one college campus to another. Like lots of new high school graduates, I thought that going to college was what I was "supposed to do." So I was driving all over Southern California, trying to collect enough credits to one day get a degree. I bounced between Cal State Fullerton, Fullerton Junior College, Cypress College, Orange Coast College, and Long Beach College. As soon as class ended at one campus, I'd jump in my truck and drive to another one. It seemed that no matter where I went, or how early I got there, the parking lot was always full. Soon, I came up with a strategy that I was sure would work. I would look for strangers walking in the parking lot, and I'd pull up, roll down the window, and say—in my friendliest voice—"Can I drive you to your car, so I can take your parking spot, please?" Sometimes this little shuttle-service routine worked. But most of the time, the person just gave me a panicked look, as if I were a creep, and blurted "No thanks!" before dashing for the safety of their car. Then I'd just drive to the next person and ask the same question, knowing eventually someone would say yes.

Meanwhile, the classes I was driving everywhere for were in subjects I cared nothing about, such as chemistry, political science, and geology. It felt like I was filling up a bingo card of requirements. But I didn't see how that bingo card would ever lead to a job, much less get me closer to my goal of material success. None of it added up for me. What I really needed was someone whose life could serve as both *inspiration* and *direction* for me. I needed a "visual" of who I wanted to be and how I could get there.

EMULATE

We've all heard the term "role model," and I want to be very clear about the difference between role models and comps. A role model is a person you admire. Maybe you decide that his or her values and behavior are worth imitating, and you might even try imitating them. But more often, a role model is nothing more than a face on a screensaver, or a poster on the wall: it's an image of a person, glamorous but remote, who may seem to have it all, but who never really becomes more to you than an attractive image. Role models have fans, but how many of those fans are actively trying to figure out *how they did it*? More importantly, how many of those fans are actually doing it?

A sure test of a comp is that you're not just admiring what they're doing; you find yourself wanting to do it, too. You're not just enthralled by that person's success in their particular field; you're not just gazing at them thinking about how wonderful their life must be. Instead, you can already feel yourself prompted to take action. It's about "operationally defining" what your comp has done: a fancy term for getting to know that person not just in terms of their public persona, but in terms of steps: how they *did* it, meaning Steps A, B, C, D, and so on.

Identifying a comp takes work. It's not about saying, "That person seems cool. That person seems to have it all." Anyone with access to the internet can do that. This is not about just "wearing the jersey." Anyone can walk around in a baseball jersey with some superstar's name on the back. If that's you, are you expressing admiration for the baseball star? If so, there's nothing wrong with that. But you can't "do" someone's image. An image doesn't tell you what steps you need to take. It's not a recipe for action.

Now consider a different reason for wearing the jersey. Imagine wearing it as a physical reminder to yourself of things like the following: "The guy whose name is on my shoulders played seven years in the minor leagues. He showed up early for practice, day after day. He gutted it out and got it done. Eventually he made 'the bigs.' That's the guy I want to be, *and I'm willing to do what he did*."

Big difference.

As of 2001, I had no heroes—role models who had achieved tremendous financial success—let alone a path for myself to get there. I knew I needed those steps, from A to B to C, but I didn't know what they were. And no one I knew could explain them to me. Instead, college counselors who didn't really know me were telling me things like, "Go take chemistry." It didn't add up.

GARY

At the time I had my "night air" revelation and committed to take a break from all the drinking and smoking, I was dating a petite brunette named Natalie. Natalie's parents were in real estate and had just bought an apartment complex out in Indio, in the desert near Palm Springs. And the more I listened to Natalie's dad, Gary, talk about business, the more excited I got. Gary Lucas was a physically imposing guy: about six feet tall and six feet wide, with sparkling green eyes, a big smile, and a voice to match. And Gary's stories about his many years in the real estate game sounded like movie cliffhangers, with Gary himself in the starring role. Pretty soon, even when the house was full of people Natalie's and my age, I would make excuses to sneak away, just so I could listen to Gary.

That summer, when I wasn't attending college classes, I was still doing what I could to make money. My best gig by far turned out to be a job selling kitchen knives. I learned the products, I perfected my sales pitch, and I got after it. For a while I was one of the top salespeople in the country. Then disaster struck.

Dedicated salesman that I was, I had been keeping a thick sales book of all my customers. It also contained the names and contact information for my new leads. Whenever I looked at it, my sales binder reassured me that I was on my way.

One afternoon—to this day, I have no idea how—I lost my binder. One moment I had it under my arm, and the next it was gone. Things got worse. I stopped by an ATM in a shopping center in Cerritos, California. I punched in the code to check my balance. What popped up on the screen felt like a punch to the gut. I was down to my last couple hundred dollars. Without my noticing it, the money had evaporated. It was time to double-check my location.

———

It's fair to say that before I met Gary, my life was full of activity. I was burning gas and taking classes and selling knives. I was busy. But it sure didn't feel to me that my busyness was directed toward an actual goal.

Looking back, I know it was only when I encountered Gary that I found myself "stirred up." I became intensely curious about an industry—real estate—that I knew almost nothing about. That's when things began to click. At first, I couldn't have said why, on those nights at Natalie's house, I found myself drifting out to the backyard. That's where Gary would be holding court, drinking vodka and smoking a cigar. At the time, all I knew was that he was interesting. I now realize that my younger self was edging closer to saying, "Pay attention! *This guy is a comp for you!*" I sensed that draw, but I couldn't have explained it. Today, with hindsight, I know how to explain it.

For starters, I could see that Gary and his wife were building substantial wealth with their real estate investments. (*Click!* That had been my dream, too—almost from the moment I'd met my childhood friend Paul.) I saw that both of them were hard workers. After learning about real estate from Gary, Natalie's mom, Irene, had created her own LLC and bought almost thirty rental houses. Now she was putting in long hours, day after day, renovating the complex in Indio. (*Click!* Hard work didn't scare me; I had grown up in an environment where it was expected.) Next,

Gary was a natural entertainer. Poking the air with his cigar to punctuate his sentences, he would build suspense, then pause for dramatic effect, then—finally—roar the punch line. Without ever leaving his favorite armchair, Gary spun colorful stories that had me spellbound. (*Click!* That was me, too: I loved cracking jokes and spinning pizza dough and doing whatever I could to entertain people, for as long as I could remember.) Also, his stories made it clear that Gary was a risk taker. More than once, he had been willing to put everything on the line when he thought the odds were good. (*Click!* There I am again: looking for thrills, looking for the next adrenaline rush.) The way Gary talked about business made the whole thing sound like a high-speed chess game, a game that demanded quick thinking under tremendous pressure—and an ability to look two or three moves ahead. (*Click!* again: if I knew anything at all about myself in those days, it was that the right kind of pressure brought out the best in me. And I loved seeing connections, figuring out how to get from Point A to B and C, all the way to Z.)

In other words, I might not have known how to say it then, but the things that jazzed Gary were the very same things that jazzed me, too. Physically, yes, he was as wide as he was tall. Parked in his recliner and surrounded by clouds of cigar smoke, he looked like a planet with its own weather systems. And yes, he was old enough to be my dad. So if you had dared to tell me then that my girlfriend's dad and I had a lot in common, I know I would have scoffed. But sometimes, your most important discoveries sneak up on you. Sometimes, your comp is sitting right next to you, and you don't even know it. But believe me, it's a lot better to be intentional about it. It's far better to go out and purposely find a comp to emulate. I was twenty, and Gary quickly became my best friend.

———

The importance of all this wasn't clear to me right away. Standing there at the ATM in Cerritos, stunned, I had no idea what to do. For a few seconds, I just looked around me, blinking in the sun.

Across the parking lot, between an Allstate insurance agency and a florist shop, was some kind of office. My eyes lingered there, because the sign in the front was crooked. I squinted at it and saw that it read, "Century 21, Wise Ol' Owl." Below that sign hung another one, a strip of yellow canvas that said, "Real Estate Classes Here."

Real estate classes.

It was a defining moment: one of those moments that change the trajectory of your life. Right in front of me was a realistically achievable—and suddenly obvious!—next step, a step that could move me in the direction of my ARV, my personal vision of success. Naturally, I thought about Gary. If I could really master the ins and outs of real estate, I would know what Gary knew, and I'd be doing what Gary did. I would be on my way to my dream.

And with that, I withdrew the last of my cash from the ATM, and I headed across the parking lot to sign up.

CHAPTER FIVE

PREPARE TO LAUNCH

"Jump, Tarek! Jump!"

I'm four years old. I'm standing on the roof of the detached garage behind our Lakewood, California, house. I have just climbed the stack of firewood that sits next to our back fence. From the top of the firewood, I have pulled myself all the way up to the top of the fence, and from there onto the garage roof. My sister, Angel, who's seven, and a couple of her friends are looking up at me from our backyard. They are cheering me on.

Far below me is a yellow patch: the last bit of grass in our mostly dirt backyard. Angel waves her arms in a flapping motion, encouraging me.

"Jump, Tarek, jump!"

I never back down from a challenge—even at four years old. I study the grass patch. And then I jump. The second my feet leave the roof, I know it's a bad idea.

It feels like I'm falling forever. I hit the ground, and suddenly, everything hurts. Total blackness alternates with stabbing flashes of light, then blackness again. Hearing my screams, my mom rushes out to the backyard.

Fortunately, I survived that experience. Mom took me to the hospital, and luckily, I got away with only bumps and bruises. I wish I could say this was a one-time experience. Angel knows me better than that, though. A few years later—I am probably ten or eleven—our family has just arrived at the Mammoth ski resort for a long-anticipated winter weekend. Our room is on the third floor of the hotel. Angelique and I gaze out our open window at the deep, deep snow below. Angel has an idea. She pokes me with her elbow. I already know what's she's thinking. That's all the encouragement I need. *What could happen?* I think. The snow is so soft and fluffy! *And there's so much of it!*

The instant I hit the snow, I disappear. I go into it like a missile. The snow closes over me like a white tomb. This time it's Angelique who yells for help. Grownups come running, but the snow is so deep they can't even figure out where I am, let alone pull me out. I shove and claw at the snow for what seems like hours. At last, I stumble out, caked in white and unrecognizable. I slap the snow off my arms and legs, grinning and doing my best to pretend that the whole thing is no big deal.

These kinds of "dumbass kid" episodes are in my distant past, where they belong. I have learned—finally—not to jump off a roof. (Angel, don't even try me!) On the other hand, the passing years have not changed my mind about one thing. Many, many times since those days, and in many other environments, I have jumped and landed safely. By that I mean I've closed deals and launched new businesses and thrown myself into ventures that, at the time, might have looked even crazier than throwing myself off a roof. But I've gone for it, and it has worked. And I've done it often enough to be convinced that when life shows you an opportunity, you've got to go for it. You've got to be willing to jump. The trick is to develop confidence beforehand about what you're doing and why. And

I've learned that nothing gives you confidence like seeing someone else jump first, successfully.

———

When I stood at that ATM in Cerritos and saw "Real Estate Classes Here" on the sign across the parking lot, my next move was clear, and I'm glad I jumped. But it was far from being an impulse move. My crossing the street that afternoon was the result of months of thinking, months of turning things over in my mind.

I had to do some zigging and zagging first before I arrived at that moment of clarity. The truth is that, at twenty, I was still learning this stuff as I went.

In fact, one night, during one of those backyard conversations with Gary, and not knowing any other way to ask it, I had put it to Gary bluntly: "Hey, I want to be rich. How do I make money?"

And Gary's response was, "Well, you know, you need to know how to invest in real estate."

"Okay, cool," I said. "How do I do that?"

"Well," Gary said, "you start by learning construction."

My heart sank. It sank even lower when Gary added this unhelpful detail: "Go get a job for a contractor."

In moments like these, you've got to have an accurate self-concept. The more clearly you know who you *aren't*, the more quickly you'll be able to make the right decision for yourself.

I instantly thought about the times my dad would bring me to his shop and let me play with the tools. My first few visits went fine, but eventually Dad and his employees and I discovered that I have—shall we say—very modest mechanical ability. Eventually, whenever I visited Dad at work, he would say, "Tarek, don't touch anything!"

Yes, it's ironic that I built a career out of renovating homes. I have no problem swinging a hammer and knocking down a wall. But mechanical,

I am not. Laugh if you want to. But I knew that about myself even then. Moreover, working a construction job, at $12 an hour, sounded like a step backward to me. The path from there to "tycoon" looked as if it would take forever. So, almost instantly, I felt the disconnect. The things about Gary that clicked for me were his quick calculations, his high-stakes gamesmanship, his love of storytelling, the deals he had done. None of that—and nothing in me, personally—involved swinging a hammer. I just knew it wasn't me. So as helpful as Gary intended to be, my first reaction was to completely ignore his advice. I knew myself well enough to know there had to be a better way.

Today, I would tell myself, "Hey, Tarek—instead of simply giving up, *dig a little deeper.*" I'd be telling my twenty-year-old self, "Keep the conversation going. See if you can work out how, exactly, Gary's interests and abilities line up with yours." If I had approached it that way, then as soon as he suggested getting a construction job, I would have told Gary the truth: "That's not for me; there's got to be a different way." *Then I would have kept pushing him for more information.* Imagine how much more productive our conversation would have been if I had asked Gary, "What exactly have you done that I can do right now?" I needed to hear some kind of operational "next step" framed in a way that made sense for me personally. If we had talked about it for just a few more minutes, I'd like to think Gary would have told me, "Okay, Tarek, you're a guy who's comfortable with risks, and you say you like math. Go learn how deals work. Understand the process of buying and selling homes. *Go get some training in real estate.*"

Later on, as you'll learn, I got smart enough to come back to Gary with specific questions, such as, "When X happened, Gary, *what did you do?*" Or, "If you were in my situation right now, how would you handle it?" Believe me, I learned to tap into Gary's expertise in the right way.

But that came later. In the moment, I didn't know enough to ask the right questions, questions that might have pointed me in a direction that made sense for me personally. I didn't yet know how to zero in on the next step to take. So—discouraged by what I heard—I sort of threw up my hands and resigned myself to being a college student. I decided that my "job" was to keep on keeping on. I kept going to class, I kept selling knives, and I kept busy at being busy. I was an unguided missile.

Today I know that my real job, in that moment, was to hunt for the overlaps between *my* temperament, abilities, and passions and *Gary's* temperament, abilities, and passions. My job was to turn that information into real-world actions I could take. By being timid—by not pushing harder for information—I failed to get the answers that I desperately wanted and needed. I got those answers eventually, but I could have saved a tremendous amount of time and frustration by getting them then.

I'll apply this lesson to myself today. I'll be the first to say that if you're looking at me as a "comp," I'm delighted, but I hope you acknowledge that there was some work involved, right? I didn't wake up one day and discover a TV show and that Rolodex of business contacts under my pillow! Yes, it's a thrill for me to connect with millions of people around the world through the power of the internet. But those results didn't happen until I took action. There were lots of steps along the way. So I hope you'd be asking, "Tarek hit it big as a flipper—*How* did he do it, and am I interested enough and committed enough *to do those same things?*"

The "how" is a big part of what this book is about. Meanwhile, you need to know that flipping houses is high risk, high reward. Flipping is definitely not for everybody. It's something you've got to have the stomach for. In fact, most real estate agents will tell you that they just don't have the tolerance for the risks involved in flipping. It is far from a sure thing, and you can lose tons of money. So whoever you might be looking at as your personal comp, make sure you understand—in detail—what it took for them to get where they are. Then ask yourself, *Can I see myself actually doing those things? Am I willing to do what they did to achieve success?*

You can't skip steps here. Let this search for information become your job! If your personal comp is alive and well, go ahead: ask these kinds of questions, straight up! "What are you doing, or what have you done, that you would suggest that I do right now?" I promise you'll do a better job of it than I did my first time out of the gate.

If a one-on-one conversation with your comp is impossible, that just means you have to find other ways to do this research. Study the internet! Read books! I've never been afraid to spend hundreds of hours researching the "how-to" of something I'm about to get started on. Either way, your job is to get answers, no matter what it takes. You've got to push for information. Don't give up until you have an action step in mind.

———

I might not have been able to put all of this into words at the time, but when I crossed that street in Cerritos and signed up for real estate classes, I was acting on information that I'd been gathering for a long time. Turns out it was great information. Now it was time to do the work.

The classes at Wise Ol' Owl went pretty much as you might expect. After I signed up, they stuck me in a tiny windowless brown-and-gold room and turned on the VCR. I found myself watching seemingly endless VHS videos from the 1980s starring women in gold jackets with huge shoulder pads. In each video, these lovely ladies slowly—very, very slowly—walked the viewer through the nuts and bolts of real estate law, ethics, contracts, and so on. Every day, it felt like school all over again. More than once I almost bolted out of there. And with hindsight, I now know that a lot of what was taught in those training sessions had almost nothing to do with representing buyers or sellers—which is how you actually make money. But I stayed with it. Looking back, I know why.

To begin with, I knew enough about *who I was, and what I wanted*, to recognize that the pain of those training classes was only temporary. I knew I could do the math. I knew I could sell, and I could see how selling houses lined up with my abilities. In fancy terms, I had enough of a self-concept in place to know that real estate was something I could do. But I couldn't do it until I got that license.

Second, I could see that there was money to be made. Understanding how deals worked and how to run the numbers on a transaction started to get interesting, even though a lot of the training never did. I began to imagine myself as a successful agent—the starting pitcher, you might say—of these deals. I started to be engaged.

Third, I had a comp—an actual person to compare myself to. My confidence about what I was doing had shot up thanks to my encounters with Gary. Gary was living proof that all the work I put into getting a license could bear fruit in a spectacular way.

To sum it all up, I understood that these classes were an all-important sub-goal if I ever wanted to reach my main goal of selling real estate. My "after-repaired value"—who I could become once I accomplished all the steps—was starting to come into focus.

MOM'S GARAGE

Not long after I started taking real estate classes, Natalie and I ended our relationship, and I no longer had a place to live. I swallowed my pride and moved back into our old family home in Buena Park. Dad had moved out, and my mom had begun renting out Angelique's and my old bedrooms to help cover her bills. Since I could no longer use my bedroom, I asked Mom if she'd let me sleep in the garage, and she laughed and said, "Yes, if you can handle it."

To explain what she meant: this wasn't a converted garage, a space that was renovated for humans to occupy. This was a *garage*, where you park your cars and store your roach killer and your Christmas decorations:

the place with the big oil stains on the floor. After my first night trying to sleep in this depressing cave, I knew I had to do something to fix the place up. So I unfolded our old cot and wedged it between some crummy paint cans and my old dirt bike. I dragged a couch and a TV out there. As a finishing touch, I tacked my snowboarding posters to the wall. *Not bad,* I thought. Definitely a step up from a bulldozed apartment. Soon, to my surprise, I was renovating not just my living quarters, but my life.

I had to share Mom's kitchen with her paying tenants. One of them was Justin. Justin and I had nothing in common except that he now occupied my old bedroom. He was a bald-shaven dude who had just arrived from Texas, and he was tatted up from head to toe. He was twenty-five, which seemed practically middle-aged to me then. I wasn't sure how I felt about him using my room, but I certainly saw no reason to spend any time around him.

A few weeks into my stay, Justin presented me with what sounded like an ultimatum. We were crossing paths in Mom's kitchen when he said to me, very casually, "Dude. You want to start working out with me tomorrow?"

Right away I started doing that mental dance you do when the Jehovah's Witnesses ring your doorbell. Didn't Justin see how out of shape I was? Hadn't he noticed my "muffin top"? Surely he understood that I had no intention of going anywhere to work out, let alone with him! But this was the brilliant comeback that I came up with: "Uh...okay. Yeah. Sure."

In case I still had any secret idea of getting out of it, Justin's next words had me pinned. "Okay," he said. "Workout. Tomorrow night. Seven o'clock." At that point, I assumed he was talking about doing a few push-ups in the living room.

The next night at seven o'clock, my life moved another degree in the right direction. After a long day at work, I arrived home, where Justin was waiting.

"Ready to work out?"

"Yeah," I said. "I've got some dumbbells in the garage." I was still assuming this would be a one-time, fifteen-minute workout. I wanted to get it over with.

Justin laughed. "What the hell are you talking about? We're going to the gym."

Instantly, I was filled with anxiety. It had been years since I'd done any kind of serious workout. I knew how bad I looked. In that moment, I resented Justin as if he were my worst enemy. But I had given him my word.

On our first visit to the gym, I walked in feeling irritated, intimidated, and insecure. We lifted weights for an hour and spent thirty minutes on the treadmill. It was a grueling hour and a half. My only goal was to survive the workout. I promised myself I would never come back.

But, as I say, I had given him my word. And the very next day, Justin was waiting for me. He was waiting for me again the day after that, and for many days to follow, at seven o'clock. His greeting was always the same: "Let's go!" And every time, I went.

And something incredible happened. For the first week, I was breathless and fat and uncomfortable. But then I started to see changes in my body. Even more importantly, I began to feel confident about myself. I felt a glimmer of hope that I could once again be who I had been. Meanwhile, I felt a surge of energy. The physical effort started to feel exhilarating. Soon I went all in. Trips to the gym became like a religious discipline for me. I wasn't going to miss a day. Pretty soon, I was the one telling Justin, every night at seven o'clock, "*Let's go!*"

This wasn't about walking on the treadmill for a few minutes. Instead, it became an hour of lifting weights that were as heavy as I could manage, then killing myself on the cardio machines until I was breathless. I began losing weight—dramatically. I started seeing my muscles again. Within ninety days, I looked like a completely different person. What had taken me years of my life to destroy, I had gained back in ninety days.

This experience, and the gratification I got from it, was transformative. Without fully understanding what had happened, I was moving closer to my ARV, my after-repaired value. On the night when I stepped out onto that porch in Cerritos, and told myself I needed to make some changes, I knew I had to eliminate the negatives from my life. *But I still needed to articulate my ARV as a positive want.*

When you adopt the "flip mindset," and you're pursuing positives, you discover that there's only so much time in the day, and you no longer have time for negatives. Sure enough, the more time I spent doing healthy, positive things, the less time I had to indulge in negative behaviors even if I wanted to.

It was that first session in the gym, after almost two years of no exercise, that caused me to frame my goals in the affirmative: *I want to keep getting stronger, feeling better, and having more energy and confidence.* Once I put that affirmative "want" into words, the physical work of lifting weights and doing all that brutal cardio became extremely gratifying. And it had all started with Justin, the least likely comp I could have imagined.

The visible results were exciting. They were dramatic, real-world results. I'm certain that if I had not seen the changes happening, I would not have been so motivated. They prompted me to keep going back to the gym every single day. But in order to get those results, I had to go all in: to give it a 110 percent effort. All those team workouts in high school had given me, quite literally, a muscle memory that was now being reawakened. And I was getting reacquainted with the power of engagement: with being so focused on doing something difficult that I lost track of time. Challenging physical effort was paying off for me in a dramatic way. Every time I left the gym, I was happier and more confident than I'd been the day before.

To this day, my body still bears the evidence of my heaviest, sloppiest days. The stretch marks that started out looking like purple lightning bolts are now so faint that they're barely visible. But today, when I look at those marks, I see them as "battle scars." They are important reminders to me of how far I've come.

SCORE

In stark contrast to my college courses, the real estate training felt like movement in the right direction. The training classes were often dull, but I could see where they were leading. I kept telling myself that other people had gone through this training and made a success of real estate; therefore, I could, too. I knew that finishing the classes, and then getting my real estate license, were necessary sub-goals on the way to something bigger. So I got the job done. I was far from a finished "flip." But the foundation was set.

The day finally came when, at twenty years old, I had my real estate license in hand. I found work at a Coldwell Banker agency in Fullerton, California. The agency was in a somewhat rundown medical building that had been converted into real estate offices. My earliest impressions were that all real estate firms must be quiet and sedate. I assumed that all real estate agents must be kindly older folks who stayed calm and professional at all times. (Other jobs, in other real estate offices, later on, changed my thinking in a major way.) Meanwhile—still believing that I needed a college degree—I kept taking classes wherever I could.

Now that I was in real estate, it occurred to me that I needed a "real estate car," something I could drive clients around in. They weren't going to be as excited about my four-by-four lifted black pickup truck as I was. An older gentleman who worked for my dad happened to be selling his baby blue 1985 Buick Park Avenue, and soon I was driving around in a car that was almost as old as I was. In some ways, it was a great client car: it was roomy and comfortable, with seats that were almost like sofas. It even had an enormous old-school telephone in it. I thought the phone was so cool, but it didn't work.

One day, at a stoplight in Anaheim, the car started hopping—just jerking up and down like a lowrider, for no reason. My client, in the passenger seat, was about to say something when suddenly the air conditioning vents started blasting us with little black chunks of something, insulation debris or maybe mold. We tried to wipe the stuff off our clothes, but ended up smearing black stains all over ourselves. I looked at my client and said, as cheerfully as I could, "I don't even know what that is, but it'll come out!"

A hard truth about working in real estate is that clients sometimes drop you and go with someone else. It's not unusual, but it's depressing when it happens. Not surprisingly, that's what happened here. A few days later I learned that the client had bought a house with a different agent. (I never did learn what that black stuff was!)

Bigger, much more serious challenges were coming. One of these challenges almost ended my real estate career altogether. In a crazy twist, however, near-disaster turned into a golden opportunity. By taking massive action, I was able to open up an entirely new path for myself.

I had settled into my new spot at Coldwell Banker, and I fully expected my phone to start ringing with potential clients. I patterned myself after what I saw other agents doing: mostly holding open houses and passing out hundreds of flyers. But none of it was working. Back then, real estate offices had something called "floor time": an agent would be assigned to sit a four-hour shift in hopes that a potential client would call on the phone in response to one of the newspaper or magazine ads that were running. Agents hated doing floor time because it was so monotonous, and because it was a difficult way to get clients. But it was one of the only ways I knew how. So I often volunteered to pick up other agents' floor-time shifts, hoping a client would call.

Months into the job, however, it came over me—almost like a wave of nausea—that nobody out there needed my help. Nobody was calling me to buy, and nobody was calling me to sell. Soon, every day followed the same pattern: between classes, I would put on one of my JCPenney suits, drive to Coldwell Banker, sit at my desk for hours, then leave.

Pretty soon, I was more than just unbelievably bored; I was on the verge of despair. I felt no engagement or fulfillment of any kind. As far as I could tell, my so-called career was stalled. There were no deals. There was no adventure. And there was definitely no money. I kept waiting, and waiting, and waiting. But nothing ever happened.

In late November 2002, the day finally came when I thought I might lose my mind. I was two hours into a four-hour floor-time shift, and, as usual, nothing was happening. I started feeling anxiety, a tightness in my chest. As the minutes ticked by, I became convinced that I was wasting my life.

That's it, I told myself. I stood up, pushed my chair under the desk, and bolted from the office. Breezing past the startled receptionist, I announced, "I quit!" Then I got the hell out of there and went home.

Flopping onto the cot in Mom's garage, I cracked open a beer, grabbed the TV remote, and settled back onto the crappy mattress, more than ready for the distraction of a football game.

A little before halftime, my phone rang. It was Carol, the Coldwell Banker receptionist. "Hey, Tarek," she said. "There's some guy here who wants to go see a house."

I thought for a moment, *You've got to be kidding me! I already accepted that I quit!* But something inside told me to get off my ass and go. I turned the game off, threw my suit back on, and dashed back to the office. I met the clients and learned that they were ready to make an offer on a house. Unusually, it was a property they already knew they wanted to buy—they didn't even want me to show it to them. And in order to buy this new house, they had to list their current house for sale. So within the hour, I had put together a contract to list their home as well as an offer for the home they wanted to buy. Once the clients left, I knew I needed to get that offer to the listing agent right away. I grabbed the paperwork and walked it over to the fax machine.

But the first page was halfway into the machine when I suddenly stopped. I asked myself, "In this market, where every listing is getting ten offers, is this the best way to get this deal done?" I quickly realized, *No, it isn't.* If the market was as hot as everyone said, then by the time I finished faxing my offer, it would be one of ten offers sitting in the agent's in-box. I knew it had to stand out.

To hell with this, I said to myself. *I'm going for broke.*

I yanked my offer back out of the fax machine and looked at the listing agent's physical address. It said "RE/MAX," and it gave the agent's name as Carl Maxson. Whoever Carl Maxson was, I had to plead my case to him in person, because I really needed to make the sale. In that moment, the thing I wanted most demanded that I take action. So I jumped into my Buick and drove straight to RE/MAX.

Located on a high floor of a new-looking office tower, with a gleaming RE/MAX logo looking down on a plush reception area, this was a far cry from the rundown Coldwell Banker offices I had just left. I walked up to the receptionist's desk and said, "Is Carl Maxson here? I'd like to see him."

Looking up from her computer screen, the young Asian receptionist asked me, "Do you have an appointment?"

"No, I don't. But I just need to talk to him really quick. I have an offer for him."

She sort of laughed, looking at me as if I were crazy.

"You can't just come 'see Carl Maxson,'" she said, as if I should know who Carl Maxson was.

Immediately—mustering a big smile and as much charm as I could come up with—I started pleading my case. (Remember, Tarek means "the one who knocks.") Then I added, "For two minutes. Just two minutes. *Please.*"

Finally, the receptionist laughed, told me I was crazy, got up, and walked down the hall. When she came back, she said, "It's your lucky day. Carl said fine, you can come back," and she pointed me toward his office.

"Last door on the left."

Heading down the hall, I felt a strange mix of emotions. Mostly I was terrified. After all, the document in my hand represented, for the moment, my client's hopes and dreams—and the opportunity for me to make more money than I ever thought possible. No pressure! But I was also filled with excitement, knowing I had a chance of scoring my first deal.

The last door on the left turned out to be a corner office that (I soon found out) was the biggest one in the building. It could easily have accommodated five people. Two sides consisted entirely of floor-to-ceiling windows, and every other inch of space seemed to be taken up by awards. Plaques and certificates blanketed the walls, and there were gleaming trophies on every shelf. Whoever this guy was, he was obviously doing something right.

Waiting for me behind a giant desk was a six-foot-tall, solidly built, bald-shaven guy with a jet-black goatee. I'm not sure what I expected, but I know I wasn't expecting the mango-orange Hawaiian shirt and the casual slacks. "Carl Maxson," he said, by way of introduction. Then he gave me a bone-crushing handshake, told me to sit down, and asked, "What have you got?"

I handed him the written offer, and as I recited the details out loud, he flipped through its pages. After a few seconds, Carl held up a hand, stopping me in midsentence. He pulled out a manila folder and one by one started showing me all the offers he'd already received on this house—which, as it turned out, was not just his listing, but also his personal home.

Then he said, "Tarek, I'm willing to take your offer—right now. Your clients can buy my house. But you, my friend, are going to have to leave Coldwell Banker. If you want me to take this offer, you're going to have to start working for me, at this agency, starting now." Then he held out his hand to close the deal with another handshake. "You have five seconds to decide."

Suddenly, everything clicked: Carl Maxson was not just the owner and listing agent on this house; he was the boss, the owner of the whole brokerage! I sat there blinking, trying to make sense of what had just happened.

Here was a guy who had found huge success in an industry I desperately wanted to thrive in. He had his own agency. Carl Maxson was clearly at the top of the real estate game, and I wanted to know how he had gotten there. And, apparently, he recognized something in me. Wasn't this the momentum I needed? I felt the seconds ticking by. Then I stuck out my hand. I heard myself say, *"Let's do this."*

As I've said, for my clients to buy Carl's house, they had to sell their house first. The next day, Carl brought a buyer to buy my clients' house. That meant that in less than twenty-four hours, I had two escrows: two properties under contract for sale. My total commission was $33,000. This was 2002, and I was twenty years old. It was a lot of money.

The whole thing was wild. It had happened so fast. One hour, I'm quitting real estate and consoling myself with a beer in my mom's garage. The next hour, I'm negotiating on a deal that could bring me a commission check far bigger than anything I imagined to be possible. Plus, I had a new job. It was another defining moment for me—something that changed the trajectory of my life. It was as dramatic as deciding to take real estate classes after seeing a crooked sign for them across a parking lot.

And it was the type of adventure I loved. I loved the intense focus of dashing back to the office, grabbing the offer, racing over to see Carl Maxson in person, selling my way in, and making it into his office. All of that excitement brought me back to my baseball days and the thrill of being up to bat in the bottom of the ninth, bases loaded. When the pressure's on, you go for broke.

———

Here's a question: When you're twenty years old, and you go from selling kitchen knives at $150 per sale to pocketing around $33,000, overnight, would it not be reasonable for you to conclude that you are extremely rich? Of course it would. Now, rich people buy nice things, right? So, wouldn't it also be appropriate for me to buy something nice for myself? Of course it would!

The very next day, I went out and bought myself a brand-new jet-black Cadillac Escalade. I drove off the lot with Tupac blasting from the surround-sound speakers. For the first time in my life, I felt like I had made it.

It turned out that the only way I could get a loan on that car was by putting down $25,000. After all, I was a twenty-year-old kid, with no credit history, buying a $55,000 car. As impressed as I was with my taste in cars, I quickly became less certain about how rich I was. I had just handed about 80 percent of my net worth to the Cadillac dealer.

Unfortunately, it wasn't long before the phone at RE/MAX started sounding exactly like the one at Coldwell Banker. It fell completely silent. A month after my big score, it hit me: I'm broke again. Gas prices had skyrocketed, and I couldn't even afford to put gas in my car. My brand-new Escalade sat there in my mom's driveway, rotting away.

As I say, I was a work in progress.

CHAPTER SIX

ENLIST YOUR CREW

Here's where things stood for me as 2002 was drawing to a close. Six months into my career at Coldwell Banker, I had struck out. The phone never rang. Then I got that lucky call and raced to Carl Maxson's RE/MAX office, where I got a strong handshake, an amazing deal, and a new job. Thanks to the deal, I had pocketed $33,000. Thinking I was rich, I had put $25,000 down on a Cadillac Escalade and spent the rest on a bunch of other crap. Now I had no business again, gas prices had spiked, I was still taking college classes, and I couldn't put gas in the car. And I was still living in my mom's garage.

In the "college of life," I had just learned three things, for sure:

First, I had learned that there was money to be made in real estate. I knew I had made a bunch of money very quickly.

Second, I knew I had no idea how to do it again! To make that money, all I had done was sit at a desk and wait for the phone to ring. In fact, at the very moment my career took off, I had just quit. How could that possibly be a recipe for success?

And third, I had learned I was broke. I had come back to a familiar place. I had forced myself into a financial corner.

Fortunately, I recognized that even though I was already a licensed real estate professional, I might need a little polishing. I knew I needed help. I committed to keeping myself wide open to new ideas. And as it happened, one day in the office I heard some other agents talking about a free seminar to be offered by some guy I'd never heard of, a real estate coach named Mike Ferry. The subject of the seminar was prospecting: how to get business. It was clear to me that these agents had no intention of going to the seminar; they were just dissing the whole concept of coaching. But I remember thinking, *Coaching? There are* coaches *for this stuff?* As someone who had been working with coaches since I was five, that intrigued me. I knew that, in sports, working with coaches, learning from them, absorbing their lessons, is how you get better. And anyway—reflecting on the sorry state of my bank account—I was more than willing to learn something, especially from anyone who might know what I needed to do to find success.

A few days later, I found myself in a ballroom at the Sequoia Athletic Club in Buena Park, one of about two hundred people there to hear from Mike Ferry. And the more Mike talked, the more fired up I got. Mike's "professor" appearance—his conservative suit and tie, his salt-and-pepper hair, his calm gestures with his eyeglasses to make a point—contrasted with the excitement of his message. It was the first time I had ever encountered a truly gifted public speaker. Mike's message that day was equal parts "hallelujah" and hard work. As exciting as he made success sound, he also made it clear that success in real estate takes effort—a lot of it. I'll never forget Mike's words: "What I'm teaching you is easy. Doing it is hard."

It felt like I'd been splashed in the face with cold water. It was invigorating. Here was information I could do something with. As Mike finished his presentation, I grabbed a piece of yellow notepaper and I wrote these words: "*You don't know who I am today, but one day you will.*" And I signed the note *Tarek El Moussa*, walked it up to the front, introduced myself to Mike, and put the note in his hand. Then I signed up for Mike's one-on-one coaching. I was hungry for direct input on whom to call, and what to say, to get new business. By the way, this was coaching that I couldn't afford. After all, I was still living in my mom's garage, and I had no money. The coaching was $1,000 a month. So out came the credit card.

The coaching focused on expired listings. When a home that's listed for sale doesn't sell during the contract period, real estate agents are notified by the multiple listing service that the contract period has ended. That means the home is no longer on the market, and a different agent can now legally solicit that seller. The challenge—and the opportunity—is to convince that homeowner to relist their home with someone else.

Mike Ferry's message was clear: expired listings are a lucrative opportunity, but if and only if you're willing to do the work it takes to become that new listing agent. I recognized who that "someone else," that new agent, should be: me. Thousands of agents would get the MLS notices, but I was determined to outwork those other agents to get those listings. I found myself thinking, *I can do this.* I was more than willing to do the work. Before the coaching ended, I had decided to specialize in expired listings. I had decided that I would succeed in real estate by taking action, rather than waiting. I would make the phone ring instead of waiting for the phone to ring.

Within days, I had set myself up with a telephone headset and a script to use for my calls to prospective sellers. My system was simple. I would allow three rings. If the prospect answered in three, after introducing myself, I was ready with my questions:

- When do you plan on interviewing another agent?
- If you sold this home, where would you move next?
- How soon did you plan on being there?
- Why are you moving to that area?
- What do you think stopped your home from selling?
- Do you think it's the agent's fault that the home did not sell, or do you think it's the market?

I'll admit, I wasn't reciting poetry. Sometimes, the person at the other end would ask me, "Are you reading a script?" And I would just say, "Thank you. I appreciate that. So when do you plan on moving?" (But yes, I was, in fact, reading the script.)

If they didn't answer at all—or if they hung up on me—I would immediately call the next number on my list. And I made that my job. Every moment that I wasn't in the gym, or sitting in a college class, I was making calls, all day long and into the night. I would no longer wait for success to find me. I was going to go find it.

My initial goal was to complete fifty conversations every day. Please note: my goal was *not* to get fifty listings. My goal was *not* to make money. My only goal was to complete fifty conversations a day. I would not allow myself to go home until I had made fifty contacts. And because I was hyperfocused on that one goal, I got listings, and I made money.

To complete that many "contacts" or conversations, I discovered that I had to make hundreds of phone calls. Overwhelmingly, the calls ended in one of four ways: with a no-answer, a hang-up, a "no," or a "hell no"—often with an extra obscenity or two thrown in. But I made it my job to reach that daily fifty, no matter what. So whenever the person hung up on me—which was most of the time—I basically said, "Thank you." The other person never heard this thank-you, but what I was saying, silently, was, "Sir, or ma'am, my goal today is to complete a total of fifty contacts. That's all I'm focused on today. So it doesn't matter that my call to you just now wasn't 'the one.' Your hanging up on me just got me one step closer to my goal. Thank you." I pushed to one side the negative result, the rejection, and I intentionally framed it as, "All right, cool. I only need a few more conversations before I hit fifty and I can go home. You got me one step closer to my daily goal. Thank you." In addition, I tried to make the physical act of dialing a little game; I would challenge myself to dial the next number even faster.

That became a ninety-day sprint of calling expired listings. I ended up listing multiple houses, getting one listing after another. Within the first two weeks, I had generated over $60,000 in future commissions. Once this happened, all I could think about was calling expired listings.

At the end of two weeks of calling, I found myself sitting in a lecture hall at Cal State Fullerton. If I remember right, it was a geology class, and I think the subject was Canadian rocks, but I can't be certain. I'll admit I wasn't really paying attention. That's because I was involved in an intense debate with myself. *What are you doing here? Is it going to be college, or real estate? Either way, it's got to be 100 percent. Either give everything you've got to real estate, or give up real estate and put 100 percent into college.*

I thought about the future commissions I had just generated in two short weeks. I weighed the commissions I was about to receive against how much effort I had put in to earn them. True, I had gotten hundreds of rejections, but within those rejections, I got some yeses. I had established a rhythm, and eventually I scored multiple wins. Sitting there, I couldn't help thinking that in two weeks, I had made a year's salary of a college graduate. And I still had three more years of college to get through! That's when I realized that the opportunity was way bigger in real estate. Right then and there, I told myself: *It's real estate, 100 percent.*

I stood up and walked out of that college classroom, and that was the last time I was ever in a class. Whatever stuff I had brought with me that day—my backpack, my calculator, my textbooks—I left it all there, in that classroom. The expression says, "Burn the boats!" and that's exactly what I did. By leaving all my school supplies there in the classroom, I intentionally made it impossible for myself to go back. This was another defining moment in my life.

Before I got to my car, my goal was to finish out the ninety days and see how far I could take it. I would eat, drink, and breathe real estate, keeping my focus on expired listings and turning myself into the most tenacious cold caller anywhere. I was going to become an expired-listings machine. When something is working, throw gas on the fire! And that's exactly what I did.

For three months toward the end of 2003, for ninety days in a row, that was my daily drill. Every day, all day, I did nothing except call expired listings.

At the end of these ninety days, I had generated $120,000 in real estate commissions. And just as with my first transaction, I couldn't believe how much money I made.

The difference was that this time, I understood how I had done it. If I didn't yet have a complete "proof of concept," at least I had a promising blueprint for what I needed to do. I had the dollars to show that my dream could come true. I understood the obstacles. And I had proved to myself that with intense tenacity, I could overcome them. Best of all, I had a repeatable process that would create income. I knew that if I could get one expired listing, I could get two, and so on, and it would never end, because expired listings would always be there. I learned that before you celebrate, you've got to know how to duplicate.

My ninety-day sprint had paid off. It worked. Finally, finally, it had all come together for me. I had already learned how powerful a "comp" like Gary Lucas could be. But now my desire to emulate Gary's success in real estate had been jump-started by an entirely different comp, Mike Ferry. Mike had inspired me not just with his own success story, but with a concrete agenda that I put into action. He had supplied me with the all-important operational steps: do this; then do that; then do the next thing. To put it another way, I didn't get up from Mike's presentation saying, "Hell of a speaker! Hell of a seminar!" and then drive home. I went back to the office and put on my headset, and I took action.

Mike had made it clear that the process would be hard. And it was. But I couldn't help wondering, "How far could this go? What if I really worked at real estate?" I was more than ready to find out. I wanted to keep going. I was hooked.

There was a time in my life when the idea of making hundreds of phone calls, then having most of them end in hostility and rejection, would have been devastating to me. It would have completely derailed my self-concept. But my "ninety-day sprint" in 2003 redirected my mindset in a dramatic way. For one thing, I went into the sprint with a crystal-clear want. I was determined to find out whether the sprint would work. For another thing, I had good reason to believe that it would. I'd already made enough in commissions to anticipate a good outcome. But there were no guarantees. And I had been warned. Mike Ferry could not have been more clear about how hard the work would be.

As a result, throughout those ninety days I clung to the belief that no amount of rejection was a statement about me personally. I refused to believe that people's hostility toward me said anything about my value. With every "No!" and every "Hell no!" I silently said, "Thank you, sir or ma'am. Thank you for letting me cross off one of my calls today. Thank you for getting me one step closer to my fifty contacts." In other words, I celebrated every contact, whether it was good or bad, because I was one step closer to going home. And eventually, I reached that goal. I saw that I could have success in real estate. Pretty soon, I was outselling everyone else in the office.

This formula—learning all I can about what to do, taking the "jump," and then doing it, relentlessly—is one that has paid off for me again and again. I've learned to tell myself, "When you never quit, you never fail. The second you give up is the second you've failed. As long as you keep trying, you're still on the road to success."

It's a flip that you just have to keep making, no matter what. You've got to believe. And you've got to surround yourself with people who have that same mindset.

———

In 1975, when my parents made the fateful decision to come to the United States, they enlisted help from my dad's brother, Mounir, whom we called Uncle Monty. Uncle Monty and his family already lived in the San Fernando Valley, just north of Los Angeles. It was Uncle Monty who sponsored my parents' visa applications and shepherded their paperwork through the immigration system. Over time, as babies were born and the family grew, Monty and Tata Lou's house became home base for all kinds of gatherings. My memories of childhood include lots of time there with my aunts and uncles and cousins. Those events were always rowdy and loud, filled with laughter, incredible smells floating from the kitchen, and the grownups shouting things in Arabic, French, and English. For a few hours, at least, my parents could simply relax and be themselves, knowing that Angel and I were fully occupied and safe and loved.

When I revisit those memories, I see all kinds of lessons about the power of relationships. I'm reminded that just a few years earlier, when rockets were flying across Beirut and my parents' apartment was destroyed, they took refuge with a large Muslim family on the first floor of their building. Days later, after a mad dash through sniper-infested streets, Mom and Dad found shelter with an Italian family who had an extra room. Very little needed to be said; both families saw that my parents needed help, and they offered it. After Lebanon, my parents' next stop was Belgium. They lived with my mom's parents until deciding to start a new life in the United States. That's when they reached out to Uncle Monty. Once they were in California, and Dad was established enough in his career to act on starting his own business, he asked a fellow employee to take the leap with him. Together they created a company that eventually employed almost thirty people.

In other words, those weekends in the Valley highlighted two facts, two equally important storylines in my family's history. One was the responsibility to work hard, to compete, and to take ownership of our results. But the other was about making sure you had the right people in your life. Competition and the will to survive mattered, but so did asking for help and giving it. Individually, my dad and Uncle Monty were high-achieving, competitive businessmen. And, like siblings everywhere, the two of them could be intensely competitive with each other. But I also saw that their relationship was full of laughter, fun, and above all, trust. They knew they could rely on each other.

When it came to raising Angelique and me, both of those messages were clear. One: work hard. Two: surround yourself with the right people. That's how our mom, after a fifty- or sixty-hour week of teaching school and after-hours tutoring, made our home the place to be on weekends. It was the best way she knew for keeping an eye on us and on the people we were spending time with. Dad was probably typical of a lot of immigrant parents in wanting me to stand out. Hollering at me at my baseball games, he demanded nothing less from me than perfection: I was expected not just to compete, but to be the best. At the same time, however, Dad recognized that I was part of a team. He understood that there were times when my teammates and I needed just to relax, to step away from the pressure for a while. So by the time we were in high school, Dad was regularly doing his best, on weekend afternoons, to create a little "Club Med" for my friends and me in our backyard. He would flip hamburgers for us and crack dumb jokes as we hung out by the pool. For a few hours, at least, we could simply spend time with each other in an environment free of any expectations.

Both of my parents were fully aware of the dangerous alternatives out there. The neighborhood where we lived was not so much white collar or blue collar as "no collar." True, the little pocket where we lived had some up-and-comers; it was where I got my first glimpse of some of the finer things in life. But it was the least rough neighborhood in a very rough area. Parts of Lakewood and Buena Park were heavily influenced by gangs. If nothing else, I was determined to conform to the gangs' sense of style. In junior high, I started waxing my hair and sleeping with a pantyhose cap on. I wanted to make sure my hair would be slicked back enough for school the next day. In the morning, I wouldn't come out of the bathroom until every hair was in place and my pants had just the right degree of "sag." Since Angelique and I shared a bathroom, this routine drove her crazy. And I lost count of how many pairs of my mom's pantyhose I cut up (but I'm sure she remembers!).

But, of course, the neighborhood gangs stood for something much more serious than a dress code. By the time I started junior high school, I was looking over my shoulder a lot. One after another, guys I knew from school got drawn into the gangs, and I saw the awful consequences when that happened. I made a conscious decision to point my life in a different direction. But first I had to survive.

At the end of my sophomore year, my parents' worst fears were realized. I was barely making Cs in school, and I had a terrible attitude. My girlfriend was a senior, and I had promised to be there on the night she graduated. That same day, however, a guy I knew learned that his girlfriend had started dating someone else. I can't remember all the details of this Romeo-and-Juliet story, but the guy was heartbroken and furious. Word got out, and soon both sides—my friend's, and the rival boyfriend's—decided that scores must be settled, immediately. Later that afternoon, about fifteen of us went to a local park, ready to fight the rival boyfriend and his friends with our fists... or so I assumed.

Minutes after we got there, it was obvious that our opponents had other plans. Two SUVs rolled up and unloaded a bunch of guys whose hands were taped up, for protection. They had baseball bats and crowbars. "Okay," I told myself, "we outnumber them—we have more bodies, but they have weapons." The two sides squared off in the middle of the park. A few words were exchanged, then mayhem erupted. Fists flew, and so did the baseball bats. During the free-for-all, an older guy—maybe nineteen or twenty—stepped toward me and swung his bat. I tried to jump out of the way, but the bat connected, hard—hard enough to break my ribs. As a reaction, I dropped my arm and knocked the bat out of his hands. I grabbed the bat and retaliated.

When I looked up, the park was a mess, all I could hear were police sirens in the distance, and all of my friends had left. There were bodies everywhere. But then, across the park, I saw that a "second wave" was gathering. And these weren't teenage boys; these were the older brothers of the guys we had just fought with. Some were obviously in their thirties. And they were running at me with crowbars. I was seventeen, and in that moment, I was all alone. That's when the police pulled up and saved my life.

I can't say for sure what happened next, but I must have blacked out. When I came to, I was sitting in the back of a police car, in handcuffs, charged with assault and battery, aggravated assault, attempted murder, and assault with a deadly weapon. Today I'm convinced that the police arrived at exactly the right moment. If I hadn't been arrested, I would have been killed.

I spent that night—the night I was supposed to be honoring my girlfriend by watching her graduate—in juvenile detention in the city of Orange. As the cell door clanged shut, I was terrified. The charges against me were very serious, and I didn't know if I was going to be there for a day, a week, or years. The cots were bare metal, and I had no idea that the bedsheets were stored inside the pillowcase, so I shivered all night, from fear and cold. Since they wouldn't let us have toothbrushes, I had to brush my teeth with a sponge.

On the second night, I got a cellmate. With his bald head, his wrinkled neck, and tattoos all over his body, he looked like he was forty—a whole lot older than anyone you'd expect to see in "juvie." He was a scary-looking dude, and he had obviously been there before. When he saw me lie down on my metal cot, he told me to look in my pillowcase for my sheets. Meanwhile, my parents, who were frantic, had reached out to an attorney and were working to get me out. After some investigation, the prosecutors figured out that I had used the other guy's bat in self-defense, during mutual combat. It helped that I had a clean record. They dropped the charges and sent me home, but I was on house arrest for about a week. I was still in pain, and it took a few weeks for my ribs to heal, but I knew I was lucky to be alive.

Shortly after this episode, a psychiatrist put me on a medicine called Dexedrine, a powerful drug that reduces impulsivity. This was the first time I'd been medicated for my ADHD, and the change I experienced was incredible. It was as if everything suddenly slowed down. I was able—finally—to focus in school. By the time I graduated, my GPA had climbed from a C average to a 3.8, almost straight As. But there were other consequences that were not so great. The doctors made me "normal" for a while, and I learned that "normal" makes good grades—but I knew something was off, and I hated it. In fact, I'm sure those early doses were fifty times stronger than the one I take today. Overnight, I went from wild-eyed, hyperactive Tarek to a guy who just sat there, stoned off his ass, saying nothing and feeling frozen. The point is that it took a while to get the dosage right, and the medication hasn't "cured" my ADHD, by any means, but I'm deeply grateful for it.

Meanwhile, I promised myself I would never end up in that kind of situation ever again. On the one hand, I've never in my life gone looking for a fight. Even in my stupid teenage years, I only fought to protect someone else. On the other hand, this whole juvie experience scared the hell out of me. Walking across the park that day, I had come face-to-face with the very worst embodiment of a "crew," and they had come very close to killing me. I saw that I would have to redirect my instinct to fight. I needed to throw myself into fights that really mattered, ones that wouldn't get me killed.

Just a few years later, one of the first things that really registered for me in my Wise Ol' Owl training course was that no successful real estate agent does it alone. It made perfect sense to me that a real estate agent would cultivate relationships with other professionals—brokers, appraisers, inspectors, mortgage lenders, title agents, and so on. As young as I was, that message instantly resonated. I understood teamwork. Later, I saw that it was just as true in the flipping world. As a flipper, I need to rely on contractors, real estate agents, appraisers, and inspectors. I need scouts to go out and hunt for properties. I need brokers to list my properties for sale and to get them sold. The skills and energy that other people bring free me up to create new opportunities, new directions for my businesses. Building and relying on teams—healthy and positive "crews," if you will—has been essential to my success.

And this "crew" approach includes asking for input or advice. Whatever the business may be that I'm working on, the more I do it, the more confidence I gain about what I'm doing. But I'm never afraid to ask for another professional's take. For example, starting out in flipping, I had no problem saying to a broker, "I think the ARV on this house is X: that's the number I think I can price it at," and asking, "Does my number sound like it's on target or not?" Ultimately, of course, the decision about whether to buy that house will always be up to me. But the basic principle holds true: I need to be confident about what I'm doing—confident enough to ask for help when I need it. I don't hesitate to invite another expert to "check my work."

The fact is that I'm constantly looking up, down, and sideways in order to get the help I need. I'm always on the lookout for new ideas, new ways of doing things. That means I'm always looking for comps, for people I want to emulate: people whose success inspires and motivates me. It's always helpful to me to learn how they did it. By "sideways," I mean I've learned how helpful it can be to align myself with other investors. There's no substitute for bouncing ideas off my peers in the industry. And I'm constantly delegating. I've never been ashamed to place myself at the head of a "crew" and then call the play. When I give clear directions to others and lay out expectations for them, all of us are in a position to help each other succeed.

BELIEVE

This chapter is about enlisting the right crew to help you flip your life, and what characteristics to look for. Let me go straight to the characteristic that I consider to be the most important by far: mindset. Mindset is what you believe about yourself, and it has a powerful effect on what you want and whether you'll succeed in getting it.

The wrong mindset says, in effect, "My life is the way it is because of things that were fixed at birth." It's the belief that I'm just a package of pre-determined things like IQ, talent, creativity, and personality. All of those are things I can't do anything about. And those things (according to this "fixed mindset") dictate my results. No matter what the situation, or what the challenge, this person believes the outcome will confirm one of two fundamental "truths" about them: it will prove either (a) that they're a winner, or (b) that they're a loser. It's the kind of flawed thinking that we looked at back in Chapter Three.

But there's a very different way of thinking about challenges, and it's called "growth mindset." The growth mindset says, I have some basic qualities, but those qualities represent potentials. *With practice and experience, I can get better at things.*

My daughter, Taylor, came home from school one day with an exciting discovery—one that's highly relevant here. She couldn't wait to share it with me. Her class had been learning about neuroplasticity, a fundamental part of how we learn. The gist is that the things you experience cause changes in the physical connections inside your brain. Throughout your life, the brain connections will reorganize and grow stronger in response to what you experience. In other words, *your experiences create anatomical changes in your brain.*

I strongly believe that I am living proof of neuroplasticity. I know that when I believe I can get better, and I act on that belief, I set myself up for more and more success. When I adopt the right mindset, I can and do get better.

In my mind's eye, it's like one of those jungle gyms you see at the play-ground, with kids climbing all over it. Some kids climb straight up; their path to the top is a straight line. Other kids start climbing, but when they discover that there's another kid above them, blocking their path, they get discouraged and quit.

Then there are the kids who climb, find the route blocked, and then move sideways a little bit, climbing some more to get to the next level. Maybe they bump into another obstacle. So they go sideways again, and up again, and so on. And eventually, they reach the top. They never stop looking for a way to go all the way up. They've learned that by making a tiny adjustment—just a horizontal step or two, to the left or the right—they solve the problem. By making adjustments, over and over, they open up a path to the top. Meanwhile, their brains are changing, making it possible for them to do this process again, faster and more confidently every time.

As long as you are moving toward your ARV—your personal vision for your better self—give yourself permission to try different paths for getting there. In other words, be persistent in your momentum, but be willing to change your method. Just as importantly, surround yourself with people who have that same mindset.

If you're not seeing the results you want, *whether from yourself or others*, the first place you want to look is mindset. Beliefs affect actions. You've got to believe!

THE TAILGATE

Picture a construction site. The contractor or crew leader rolls up in a pickup truck, drops the tailgate, and calls a meeting. Together, the team maps out what needs to be done that day. They talk about who's going to do what. This tailgate conference establishes the agenda and priorities for the day. It's an opportunity to air out problems and talk through solutions.

Consider the people in your life who would jump into action for you when you most needed help. These are the people you can count on to say, *How can I help?* and *What's the plan?* If you called a tailgate, who would show up? Can those people count on you to show up at theirs?

In order to enlist the right crew for yourself, you've got to embrace the principle of reciprocity: you need to bring value to the equation. If you hope to rely on other people, lean on them, and learn from them, then you need to show them they can rely on you. In some ways, that's the easy part. The much harder part—for guys, especially—is asking for help. We insist on going it alone. We bottle things up. I get it.

Even as a kid, I understood that my actions had outcomes. And for better or worse, I saw that most things that happened to me were because of...me. It took years of participating on teams for me to understand that people are born to collaborate. Later in life, I went through a series of crises—and there were plenty of them—when I absolutely had to ask for help. My survival depended on having a "crew." But I know that, at times, I've fought against asking for help.

I guess there's something especially "male" about this tendency. Men fear being ashamed or humiliated in front of other men; we dread being "exposed" as not measuring up. I think we view reaching out and asking for help as a confession of weakness. But the fact is we all need teammates. Remember: The growth mindset is not about constantly "going it alone." It *is* about constantly looking for ways to keep going—*which includes being willing to ask for help.*

An example of all of this comes immediately to mind: someone you've already met. My friendship with Ronnie Skyberg, my Newport Beach roommate, dates back to our time together playing high school baseball. Ronnie worked his way up the pitching roster, and by our senior year he was the starting pitcher for Sunny Hills High. He finished the season as the MVP of our entire league. By then I had long since given up any hope of pitching, but I did what I could to cheer Ronnie on. Long before that, we had quit being rivals for the starting pitcher job; we were simply teammates and friends. Not being able to pitch was painful to me, but what was more important was encouraging Ronnie whenever he was on the mound.

The next year, when that Bobcat rolled up to our apartment in Newport Beach and bulldozed the walls, Ronnie began the process of flipping his own life. The destruction was a wake-up call for him. He adopted the flip mindset in a big way. Ronnie did some "self-inventorying"—some evaluation of himself—and realized how much satisfaction he got from helping people. Looking around for inspiration and direction, he realized that one of his "comps" had always been his uncle, a captain in the fire department. The more Ronnie learned about a firefighting career, the more attractive it looked; he saw that he could make a career of helping people. And so he took massive action. He found a new place to live, worked his way through the fire academy, and got hired as a firefighter by the City of Palm Springs. I threw a graduation party for him. Just a few years after that, Ronnie was ready to make another "upward jump." After a grueling program of self-study, he qualified as a paramedic. He proved to himself what he was capable of.

And as I've already noted, my career as a flipper really took off when I enlisted other people to help. I'm talking about people like Adam Lindholm, people who understood the business opportunity and were willing to join forces with me. They, too, experienced the incredible changes that come when you adopt the right mindset. Later—as you'll learn—in the midst of my terrifying health scares, it was people like these, the guys I consider my "crew," who stepped in and got me through it.

I've never been afraid to work hard, but one of the things I work hardest at is working smarter. And one of the best ways to work smarter is to get help. I always look for shortcuts. If you leverage other people's knowledge, you'll go much further, and you'll get there faster.

———

When it comes to assembling a crew of your own, here are characteristics to look for:

Mindset. As I hope I've made clear, if you could choose only one characteristic for the people you want on your crew, this is the one. Be very cautious about putting too much emphasis on traits like "smart" or "talented." The fact is that there are plenty of people who are smart enough or talented enough to accomplish what you need. But will they? You want people around you who are willing to work as hard as you are. Look for evidence that they're willing to scramble up that jungle gym, even when the path seems blocked. Look for people who can stick with it—and with you!—through good times and bad.

Constructive cheerleading. When things get tough, we all need cheerleaders. But the best cheerleaders do more than say, "Attaboy! You can do it! You're great!" That kind of generic encouragement doesn't really work. Not for very long, anyway. It's not specific; it says nothing about you personally. It may give you some short-term momentum, but that's all.

Instead, you want "constructive cheerleaders." A constructive cheerleader says *specific* things that enable you to take a small, *specific* step in the right direction. They say things like, "I know you're good at that, *because I've seen you do it*. So let's go do it." They may not know everything about you, and they don't have to be a trained counselor, by any means. But all of us need somebody who knows us well enough to say, "Look, remember that time you benched 300 pounds? Maybe you don't feel like trying 325 today—but you've gotten damn close. So we know you've got it in you! Let's go give it a shot!" You may need to ask your "cheerleaders" to give you that kind of specific feedback.

Specialized expertise. In some respects, this is the easiest category to identify. This person is a trained specialist. This crew member might have a license or professional credential you don't have. They might be an attorney, physician, counselor, or accountant. Just know that their expertise and training don't automatically qualify them for your crew. You're still looking for that growth mindset! There are plenty of professionals out there with a fixed mindset. Those are the ones who will take your money and give you very little in return. Demand better.

Complementary tools. A complementary crew member completes or adds to your project by having a knack for work that you personally could never feel any engagement in. You might be able to do their work, but you know you wouldn't want to.

For example, at a real estate closing, the escrow officer or title agent is the person who coordinates all the paperwork. They make sure the documents get sorted, signed, and filed. I suppose I could do those things if I had to, but for me it would be torture. Organizing all those documents would never, ever put me "in the zone" of focused, gratified attention. (If anything, I would "zone out"!) But this paperwork is critically important to what I do. And great title reps have a zest for it. So look for crew members who find engagement in activities that matter to what you're doing, even though those things may not be your particular version of a thrill ride.

An independent perspective. Sometimes, your best crew member is someone who has no personal interest or investment in what you're doing. For example, when I'm doing a flip, and I come up against a foundation problem with the house, I could ask the general contractor to evaluate it—but that would shift him away from whatever he's doing, and it may end up costing me more than hiring an independent expert to take a look. "Independent experts" can have biases, too, though, and what I need is an expert who will give it to me straight: a foundation company might want to sell me their most "deluxe" repair, and overestimate the problem, whereas an engineer who doesn't even perform foundation repairs may give me a more accurate, less biased opinion. Because the engineer is focused on that one issue, and not distracted by other considerations—such as how much they can charge for the repair—they will probably be the better choice. Once I understand what the foundation needs, I can hire the right people to complete the repairs.

It's an issue to be aware of with your family members and friends. Because they're so involved with you personally, they may or may not tell you what you really need to hear. They may be too invested. The point is that a certain amount of "emotional distance" can be a good thing. Your best resource may be a third party who has no connection to or investment in what you're doing.

Outspokenness. This is a trait that you want all of your crew members to have. Picture an electric utility crew, meeting at the tailgate to figure out how to deal with a downed power line. Now imagine one of them is listening to the plan and thinking, *This plan won't work. It's incredibly dangerous. But I'll just keep my mouth shut.* People could get killed!

The best tailgates encourage disagreement. Friends or not, professional experts or not, I want people around me who have both the knowledge and the guts to say, "Tarek, I think you're making a mistake." Likewise, you want people on your crew who (1) have valuable things to say, and (2) will say them. Let them know you want them to speak up—even when it means disagreeing with you.

Ultimately, it's about not just the relationships you have in your life, but the *quality* of those relationships, and whether they add to or subtract from your lasting happiness. Lasting happiness is about long life, good health, laughter, and satisfaction—yours and mine. The test of a great "crew" is that you're working together to create the conditions that make those things possible, both in your life and in the lives of the people around you.

CHAPTER SEVEN

DUPLICATE

PROOF OF CONCEPT

Not long after starting at RE/MAX—this was in late 2003—I got the listing for a three-thousand-square-foot, five-bedroom, $800,000 home in Orange, California, overlooking Anaheim Hills. The seller was a guy by the name of Josh Merrick. Tall, muscular, and only twenty-eight years old, Josh was already a self-made millionaire. Viewing the house with Josh, I was dazzled.

To use a technical term I learned in high school, the house was *badass*. It sat at the end of a cul-de-sac behind a driveway long enough for eight cars. Just inside the front door and to the right was a three-hundred-gallon aquarium swirling with restless leopard sharks. Upstairs was a bedroom made to look like a dungeon: all the walls were metallic gray and silver, and they could have passed for solid iron. The primary bedroom, down the hall, was easily twice the size of the garage I lived in. To top it off, Josh had significantly upgraded the primary bathroom. It had an eight-person Jacuzzi tub, travertine walls, and a plasma TV built into the wall.

As we were pulling out of the driveway, I blurted, "Man, I love this house—it's so cool!"

Josh looked at me and said, "Why don't you buy it?"

I felt a jolt of adrenaline. My immediate thought—of course—was, *Dude, I'm living in my mom's garage. How in the world would I ever buy this thing?* I had been hoping to have a house of my own someday. In fact, I'd already been talking to a mortgage lender I knew. He had told me the biggest loan I could qualify for was $300,000.

But in that same moment, I did some mental math. If I bought the house, the 4 percent commission coming back to me, as the agent, would be $32,000. Meanwhile, I guessed that my monthly mortgage payment would probably be about $4,000. That meant I could live "rent free" for eight months.

Next, I thought about the house's other four bedrooms: bedrooms that I wouldn't be using. I remembered that my mom had taken in tenants. Why couldn't I have tenants, too? If I did that, and if each tenant paid me $600 a month, I'd be making an extra $2,400 every month that I could use to pay the mortgage.

Meanwhile, my expired-listing work was paying off. I now had a plan, a repeatable system for making money. And even though not all of the commissions had come in yet, I believed my deals would close, and I gambled on myself that I would be able to afford this house. In other words, I could see the next step, and it was realistically achievable. This wasn't like the Escalade, something I was eager to buy before I knew if it made sense. I crunched the numbers, and the numbers worked. Before we even made it out of the driveway, I looked at Josh and said, "Well, if you can find me a loan, I'll buy it."

Josh made some calls on my behalf, but those didn't work out. Eventually, on my own initiative, I found myself talking to a mortgage lender who was very well known in the industry, a guy with the unusual and very promising name of Pete de Best. Pete ran my numbers and came back with what I wanted to hear. Not only could he get me a loan for the full $800,000, he could get me the loan on better terms than anyone else.

Waking up that morning, I hadn't even imagined buying a house. Now I was moving from a cot in my mom's garage to my very own, almost-million-dollar home. I thought I had made it.

GETTING TO KNOW PETE

Occasionally you're fortunate enough to have a personal "comp" who also joins your crew. As a comp, that person has already helped to inspire and activate your overall mission. Then they go the extra step of asking you, *How can I help?* They offer to participate in what you're trying to accomplish. When that happens, it's like winning the lottery twice. Incredibly, this kind of "double jackpot" happened for me twice in the same year.

Months before buying my home, I started becoming uneasy about my work situation. I began to think it was time for me to part ways with Carl Maxson. My constant grinding away at the expired-listings business had made me—and Carl—good money, but it had also distracted me from noticing a serious deterioration in the culture of that office. Put simply, I looked up one day and discovered that Carl's values no longer matched mine. I could see that he had become focused on a purely short-term vision. He was all about the quick buck, the kind of profit that's made by doing whatever it takes. Some clearly dishonest practices had crept into the way Carl was doing business. Real estate is a tightly regulated industry, and I was deeply worried. I saw that staying there would destroy my self-respect, and it might even cost me my license and my career.

Fortunately, word had gotten around about the kid at RE/MAX who was making a success of prospecting. I reached out to a broker named Brian Green. Brian was a young hotshot who had achieved tremendous success and had a real estate company of his own. I thought I could learn from Brian. He told me he needed someone who was good at outbound calling. I had been on his radar for a while, and he wanted me to come aboard, which I did. That decision turned out to be a great one, but not for any reason I could have expected. Instead, it jump-started one of the most important relationships of my life.

Brian leased space in a rather dumpy office building, and it turned out that the mortgage company on the same floor was the one owned by Pete de Best. Because we shared a floor, the real estate agents routinely walked over to Pete's office to see whether Pete's loan officers could get our buyers qualified for loans. But even though we crossed paths a lot, and Pete had helped me with my own loan, I can't say that Pete and I had an instant connection. Pete was and is the kind of person who favors thinking over talking. He prefers a high degree of organization over improvisation, and he's not in the habit of chasing after thrills. Tall and lanky, square-jawed, and extremely reserved, Pete was quite a contrast from the flashy personalities I'd grown used to being around.

Not long after I started working with Brian Green, I learned that we were moving to a new office. And it turned out that our new location was in a building owned by—Pete de Best! I remember thinking, Wait a second: *Our Pete?* The young guy over there, just steps from my cubicle? He can't even be ten years older than I am. How is it even possible that he could buy his own office building? I couldn't believe it.

Move-in day for any firm can be as chaotic as the first day of seventh grade. It's often a "land grab" as people stake their claims to what they think are the best offices. The competition can get childish. But on the day of our relocation, our new landlord—Pete!—waded calmly through the chaos, doing his best to make sure everyone ended up satisfied with their spots. He kept his cool and maintained an air of quiet professionalism. And as I unloaded boxes and got familiar with the impressive new space, my amazement grew. Here I was, a relative nobody, and this young guy owned a forty-thousand-square-foot, multimillion-dollar building! I remember thinking, *Damn! I need to get to know this guy.*

Immediately, I identified Pete as a comp. I set out to get an answer to that all-important question: What is this person doing, or what have they done, that I can do right now?

The process of getting to know Pete took some time. Professionally, the relationship was great. As always, our two firms often shared clients, and there was constant back-and-forth between our office and his. My fellow agents and I referred home buyers to Pete all the time. Nevertheless, many people I worked with at Brian Green were a little scared of Pete. It wasn't just that his demeanor was and is more sober and serious than "warm and fuzzy." It was that, thanks to the move, almost all of us now thought of Pete as "the big guy," the owner, the boss. Without meaning to, at all, Pete had become intimidating.

I knew I had to get past that. And I figured I had three things going for me. First, Pete was an obvious comp for me; I realized I couldn't afford *not* to get to know this young millionaire and to understand how he had done it. Second, by this point in my life, I was consciously trying to practice a growth mindset. And a growth mindset says, *What's the worst that can happen? I'll try it!* And last not but not least, Tarek means "the one who knocks," right? So every time I had the opportunity, I made a point of saying hello to Pete. Whenever we crossed paths—anytime we happened to be working a deal together—I did whatever I could to get past a simple "Hi." I worked to keep the conversation going. And ultimately, with time, I earned the privilege of learning Pete's personal story. To me, it speaks volumes about the power of the growth mindset.

———

Very early in his life, Pete developed a clear picture of the stark difference between "having" and "not having." Pete was just a kid when his parents divorced, and his mom—up to that point a full-time housewife—suddenly had to go to work to help support Pete, his two older brothers, and his sister. Pete's mom knew how to type, and she found work as a secretary making $7 an hour. Pete's dad was a janitor. Whenever his dad couldn't work a particular shift, he would enlist one of Pete's brothers to cover for him. In turn, Pete's brothers sometimes grabbed little Pete to help out. Pete discovered that cleaning toilets and emptying trash cans at two in the morning is about the most motivating thing you can ever do in your life.

One of Pete's first great "flips" in life was actually one he helped his mom accomplish. He knew his mom desperately wanted to quit her secretary job and become a teacher. He also knew she could never pass the qualifying exam for her teacher's license because she wasn't proficient in math. So Pete—who was really good in school, especially math—appointed himself his mom's math tutor. For weeks before the big exam, Pete worked with her, and worked with her, and ultimately, she passed. She got her teacher's license. And the family's financial situation improved dramatically. Living on a teacher's salary didn't mean they were suddenly rich, by any means. But they were no longer struggling to get by on his mom's $7 hourly wage. It's the kind of "flip" that can cause a fixed mindset person to grasp, forever, the power of a growth mindset. It's living proof that hard work is the thing! Hard work pays off!

I discovered something else that I had in common with Pete. More than once I've found myself backed into a corner—a crisis—and on the verge of panic. Yet time after time, those crisis moments have turned into amazing wins. What started out as a panicky "flop" becomes an incredible "flip." I lose my sales book, I discover the near-zero balance in my bank account—and I jump into real estate. I buy a brand-new car, discover I can't afford to drive it, and now I have no choice but to make a success of specializing in expired listings. You look back at those crisis moments and, as incredible as it seems, you say, *I'm really glad that happened.*

Pete's "glad that happened" moment came when he found himself in college and enjoying himself a little too much. Apparently, he had loosened up so much that he was on the verge of flunking out. He was summoned to a meeting with the head of his academic department, who laid it all out: Pete's GPA was terrible. The situation was dire. And sitting there, trying not to panic, Pete thought back to his childhood experiences as an "assistant janitor." He remembered, in vivid detail, what it had been like to clean toilets—the disgust and embarrassment he had felt, his determination to have something better in his life. And before Pete left that meeting, his "flip" was already underway. He had found his motivation. Starting that afternoon, he worked his way to a perfect 4.0 GPA, and he made the dean's list the next quarter.

When Pete graduated and decided to go into the mortgage industry, plenty of big-name banks offered him mortgage lending jobs—at $13 an hour or so. Pete wasn't having that. He was determined to get paid what he knew he was worth. So he elected to take a job that paid him entirely on commission. Then he threw himself into the work.

And now, just a few years after making that bet on himself, Pete's results were all around me, in the form of that beautiful, sleek, multimillion-dollar office building. It was spectacular proof of the growth mindset. What you believe about yourself has a powerful effect on what you want and whether you'll succeed in getting it. You've got to believe.

———

By the end of 2004, once again, I felt like I was in a corner—and, once again, it had a lot to do with the leadership of the agency where I was working. But, once again, being forced into a corner created a whole new opportunity. It opened a door to something far better than I could have imagined.

As much as I liked being around Pete de Best, things were different when it came to my actual manager, Brian Green. I had started the Brian Green job fully intending to scale up. Brian had encouraged me to hire people to work for me, to create a kind of "Team Tarek." At long last, I was empowered to enlist my own crew. We agreed that I would train them how to prospect and work the way I worked. Once my crew was up and running, my team members would start to make the kind of money I had been making, and by taking a cut of the action, I would wind up way ahead. Everyone would be happy. Instead, over time it became clear to me that Brian had a plan of his own. I brought guys in and trained them, only to discover that, as soon as they became good at what they were doing, Brian would manipulate them to work for him instead. Déjà vu: once again, I felt like I was making good money for some pretty bad people.

At that time, the real estate agency widely considered the best in that part of Southern California was Prudential California Realty in Anaheim Hills. Prudential had a stellar reputation for professionalism. Its agents were heavy hitters, and it had become one of the most successful franchises in the Prudential network. Compared to where I was working, Prudential was the major leagues. I decided that Prudential Anaheim Hills was where I needed to be, and that it was time to work at a professional office.

The managing broker at Prudential was Brad Pearson. And Brad wouldn't return my calls. Well, if I had learned anything in my career up to that point, it was that if you want something to happen, you don't wait for it. You act. So just before Christmas of 2004, I jumped in my car and went to see Brad.

As I expected, Prudential's offices took up an entire floor of a deluxe building. Stepping off the elevator, I was met with a spectacular view, through floor-to-ceiling windows, of the lush neighborhood of Anaheim Hills. As I expected, most of the people working there appeared to be significantly older than I was. I announced to the receptionist, "I'm Tarek El Moussa, and I'm here for Brad Pearson." Just like at RE/MAX, I had no appointment and I just showed up. A few minutes later, through persistence and luck, I was shaking hands with a youthful-looking blue-eyed blond guy, compact and trim and wearing a beautifully tailored suit.

I started the conversation like this: "Dude, I've been trying to reach you."

He eyed me a little cautiously. "I know, Tarek. Frankly, I never called you back because of the places where you've worked. I know how agencies like those operate."

It was just what I had feared. The reputations of Carl Maxson and Brian Green were contaminating. Once again, I was in a corner.

"None of that has anything to do with me," I said. "I'm legit. I'm the real deal. I go by the book. And I'll prove it to you. That's why I'm here, to get away from those other guys."

Brad seemed receptive. He didn't kick me out, anyway. In fact, he motioned me into his office, where we continued our chat. I told Brad that I had wanted to work at Prudential for a long time, I was a top producer, and he needed to hire me. Before I left, I had a new job.

———

Never judge a man by the seriousness of his conservative, well-cut suits. Brad Pearson turned out to be not just an excellent businessman, but a truly funny and creative guy. Like Pete de Best, Brad would eventually become a close friend and an enthusiastic supporter of the *Flip or Flop* enterprise. And, just like Pete, he embodies the growth mindset.

As I got to know Brad, I learned that his high school years had been mainly about survival. Witty and smart-mouthed and always ready with a joke, he sometimes talked his way into situations that he then had to talk his way out of, in a hurry. At 5'9" and 120 pounds in high school, he had to become an expert negotiator just to avoid getting beaten to death by the bigger kids.

Brad's father was a plumber, and his mom helped run their little plumbing business from their home. The Pearsons weren't poor, but they weren't wealthy by anyone's definition. College was out of the question for Brad—there wasn't any money for college—so he signed up for the Air Force. He set his sights on becoming an air traffic controller. He had a problem, though. His scores on that section of the military's aptitude test weren't high enough for him to be a controller. That meant he'd have to settle for whatever role the Air Force slotted him into. And Brad—just like Pete on the day Pete graduated from college—didn't want to settle. Sitting between Brad and his dream job was the recruitment officer in charge of career selection.

She gave Brad the bad news. "I'm sorry. With these scores, I just can't do it."

And Brad—aged eighteen and feeling cornered—leaned forward and made his pitch.

"Ma'am," he said, "at some point in your life, somebody gave you a chance. Somebody did something that completely changed the direction of where you were gonna go. That's what I'm asking you to do for me. I've got perfect vision, perfect hearing, and my scores aren't horrible. If there's anything you can do—anybody you can call—it would mean everything to me."

The recruiter looked at Brad, then stepped out of the office for a moment. When she came back, she was carrying a little rubber stamp. "All right," she said, stamping a document. "You've got to promise me one thing. You've got to make it through the training program." And she stamped another document, then handed the packet of papers to Brad.

"You've got to graduate," she said. "The washout rate for controllers is over 90 percent. It's really bad. And it costs the Air Force a lot of money to train people. So it's on me if I put somebody in there who shouldn't be, right?"

And true to the promise he gave the recruiter that day, Brad didn't fail. Of the twenty-odd people in the class when he started, he was one of only three to graduate. Just a few months later, still not yet nineteen years old, he was guiding fully armed B-52 bombers in the Gulf War. Brad had always been a quick thinker, but now he had to dial his "cognitive horsepower" to another level. Now he was talking to airplanes going five hundred miles an hour, and he was thinking about not just a pilot's next move, but his next four or five moves.

Once he got into real estate, this hyperfast thinking served Brad well. He learned to anticipate the moves of business competitors rather than pilots. And Brad was great at it. Without a college degree, without knowing the "big words," as he put it, Brad Pearson built a little Prudential startup into one of the biggest franchises in the country. And he had done it before he turned thirty.

On the day I showed up unannounced and asked to see him, I'd like to think that Brad saw some of himself in me. Maybe he saw the same kind of drive and ambition—desperation, maybe?—that had powered his own success. Certainly my "want" that day was as big as his had been when he sat down with the Air Force recruiter. In any event, I walked out of there with a job. And once again, I had found someone I wanted to emulate.

Within days, I knew that moving to Prudential Anaheim Hills had been the right call. In stark contrast to my previous two managers, Brad was a giver, not a taker. He freely shared his knowledge and ideas with everyone in the office, and his generous spirit kept morale high. The time felt right for me to take another run at my "Team Tarek" idea.

So, with Brad's blessing, I put together a new "expired-listings" team. I taught my guys the basic two-step: (1) Do the research to identify homes other agents had listed but couldn't sell during the period of the contract; then (2) do everything possible to get that listing. I explained that we were going to be cold-calling expired listings every morning using the script I had written. Then, in the afternoons, we would go from house to house, knocking on doors to try to get people to relist their homes with us. At night, it was back to the phones until 8:30 p.m. I told my team that my script would work if they could keep homeowners on the phone longer than three seconds. Privately, I knew that was a big "if." What I understood well—but my team could only learn from experience—was that lots and lots of rejection and disappointment were coming before we found success.

Brad gave us cubicles, but that didn't last very long. We were constantly on the phone, and we could get loud. Meanwhile, again with Brad's consent, my team's typical "uniform," when we weren't face-to-face with clients, was shorts, a T-shirt, and a baseball cap. So our arrival at Prudential was a bit of a culture shock for the tailored "grownups" around us. Frankly, if we'd stayed in cubicles, the other agents probably would have killed us. But Brad, always smooth, knew immediately how to keep the peace. He stuck all four of us in a private office, out of sight and out of earshot. We proudly referred to our shared space as the "bullpen." Brad called it the "dorm room."

Eventually, the team concept started to click. Soon, as the head of "Team Tarek," I was one of the top sellers in the Prudential office. I was on a roll.

NEW AGENT

In May 2005, a young woman arrived at Prudential fresh out of San Diego State and ready to start her career. Because of the crazy hours I was working, it took a while for the two of us to meet. Her name was Christina Haack. Christina was from the neighborhood; she had grown up in Anaheim Hills. Now she was on board, real estate license in hand, trying to become a successful agent.

If the long, monotonous first months I had spent at Coldwell Banker taught me anything, it's that your early days in a real estate career can be a rude awakening. Sure enough, that's what happened for Christina. She held open houses every weekend. She distributed marketing flyers for several hours every day. She showed properties. But none of it was paying off in the form of actual sales. Boredom and frustration were setting in for Christina, just as they had for me when I started.

Finally, Christina went to Brad Pearson for advice. "You might try working with Tarek," he told her. I guess I hadn't made much of an impression yet, because Christina's response was, "Who's Tarek?" Brad explained who I was, told her I had several people working with me, and said I was finding huge success going after expired listings. Christina agreed to give it a try, so Brad set up a formal interview.

On the day of our appointment, I could see that my new candidate had the potential to add glamour to the team. An eye-catching blonde just a few years younger than me, Christina could turn heads just by walking into a room. Now it was time to see whether she could turn opportunities into sales.

As the interview progressed, the similarities between Christina's history and mine became apparent. Like me, Christina had grown up in a family that raised her to be supercompetitive. Both of us had parents who had pushed us hard to excel in sports. At her soccer games, Christina's dad would run up and down the sidelines to make sure she wasn't "dogging it," as she put it. When she wasn't playing soccer, it was all basketball all the time. In the summer, when she would rather have been at the beach with her friends, her dad sent her to basketball camps. On weekend mornings, when most high school kids were sleeping in, Christina was out the door by 6:00 a.m. to go to a private basketball trainer in Newport Beach.

In other words, Christina's story sounded familiar. Her dad pushed her to be the best in sports—and in life. Her experience of youth sports—like mine—was not a case of being told to have fun and do your best. Instead, like me, she was expected to dominate. For better or worse, the way we'd both been raised meant that simply going through the motions had never been an option for us. We had been taught to will ourselves to ever higher levels of achievement.

Another similarity that stood out for me was Christina's love-hate experience of college. Inspired by the Tom Cruise movie *Jerry Maguire*, she had flirted with the idea of becoming a public relations rep for athletes—helping sports figures deal with the media. This mixture of PR and sports had sounded to her like the perfect recipe for an edgy, rewarding career. So when she arrived at San Diego State, she declared her major as communications, with an emphasis in public relations.

Before long, however, she discovered that her classes were not nearly as exciting as she had hoped. And that, too, sounded familiar. When you leave high school with a clear ARV, a well-defined vision of your future, and it's in a field like medicine, engineering, or law, to name a few—then college is essential. You've just got to get that "entry ticket" of a college degree before you can play. In those fields, the growth mindset you need to have is, *I'll plow through these courses, and I'll learn what I need to learn about the field, and only then will I be in a position to seize my dream.*

But a lot of people start college with no particular dream in mind. They're not focused on a specialized field. Moreover, they haven't actively looked around for a comp. So there's no one out there who fires their imagination and inspires them to take steps in a particular direction. When that's the case, college quickly starts to feel like something you're doing just because you're supposed to.

And that had been true for Christina, as it was for me. She, too, had reached a point where she decided that college classes might not be the best way for her to get real-life skills, practical knowledge that she could put to use right away. Meanwhile, she had always been interested in real estate. Her best friend growing up, Megan, was the daughter of a real estate agent. Often the two girls would tag along when Megan's mom visited open houses. So even as other career ideas came and went, Christina kept coming back to the idea of becoming a real estate agent. She had earned her real estate license while still in college. Now, in her first job, harsh reality had set in. Like me, she had discovered that you don't just walk into an agency or an open house, sit down, and immediately start selling homes.

I wasn't much older than she was, but on the day we met, I had almost three years of experience, and I was closing in on becoming one of the top agents at the Prudential office. Candidly, though, I'm not sure any of that mattered to Christina that day. It's more likely she was thinking, *Anything is better than what I'm doing now!* In any event, at the end of the interview, I invited her to join Team Tarek, and she accepted.

———

Nothing in Christina's life had prepared her for working expired listings. If anything, it probably felt even more grim than sitting in an open house all day and having nothing to show for it. After all, you're making phone calls to people who are already stressed out and being harassed by other real estate agents. They're frustrated that their homes have been sitting on the market for months and haven't sold. In many cases, they're mad at their real estate agent and the entire real estate industry. And here comes a call from another agent. To paraphrase Mike Ferry, the "how" of expired listings is easy; actually doing it is hard.

On one of her first solo calls, Christina was friendly and professional and followed my script, but it didn't matter. The prospective client hung up on her. I saw how demoralizing it was for her. For a moment, I thought about coaching Christina on what had just happened on the call. Maybe I should walk her through what she could have done differently. Instead, I thought, *What the hell*, and I picked up the phone and called the same number. Within a few minutes, I had landed Christina's first listing appointment. That afternoon—one of our first times working together outside the office—Christina and I drove together to the appointment. We were talking to the couple selling the house when both of them gave us a funny look. Then, totally out of the blue, the husband said to us, "You guys should be together."

Since both of us were dating other people at the time, it took us a while to acknowledge the connection. It took some additional time to sort everything out. Finally, though—in the fall of 2006, a little over a year after we met—we went out for drinks, telling ourselves and each other that it was to "talk about work," but we both knew better. Before long, we had ended our previous relationships and moved in together.

And that was the beginning of a wild adventure and years of extremes. Ahead of us were plenty of moments of celebration. But for all of the amazing highs, there were just as many devastating lows—including more than one major crisis. Looking back, I see this next phase of my life as a lesson in relentless renovation.

CHAPTER EIGHT

RENOVATE RELENTLESSLY

When Christina and I met, I was driving a Mercedes S500 Brabus and living in the mansion I'd bought near Anaheim Hills. Within months after we moved in together, I had to sell them both. In fact, the two of us had to sell almost everything we owned.

People talk about the Great Recession of 2008, but I can assure you that it really started in 2006. The first sign was a huge increase in the inventory of homes for sale, and an even bigger decrease in the number of homes that were actually selling. It was the perfect storm. When the market was hot, nine out of ten homes were selling. Suddenly, the number was more like one out of thirty. The earliest tremors of this disaster were happening within a twenty-mile radius of our office in Anaheim Hills. Almost overnight, it felt like every house in Orange County was in fore-closure. By late 2006, even Brad Pearson—normally a picture of upbeat, calm control—was walking around the office looking shell-shocked. Brad didn't need to say it in words. His facial expression said it all: *"We're done. We're done."* And 2007 was even worse.

In the spring of 2007, the subprime market crashed. Lenders were no longer giving mortgage loans, for zero down, to people with low credit and not much job history. Almost overnight it became much harder to get financing. At that point, there were even more homes for sale, with even fewer buyers, because they couldn't get financing. That's when the huge defaults on mortgage loans began. Banks started going out of business. But owners weren't dropping their prices. Suddenly, nothing was selling; there were massive declines in home sales. This shock wave of foreclosures and falling prices spread around the world. Plenty of homes were for sale, but no one was buying them. And even if they wanted to, they couldn't get financing.

Every day, I worked as hard as I ever had. I was still working seven days a week, putting in twelve- to fourteen-hour days, knocking on doors, and hitting the phones and calling hundreds of expired listings, as usual—but the world had gone dark. Nothing was working, literally nothing. I was still getting listing appointments, but sellers were still looking at the past—old comps—rather than realistically looking at today and the future. The typical seller I was dealing with would insist on a listing price of $800,000 when I knew the house was only worth $600,000. Time after time, I would show up to a potential listing and find myself debating with the seller over the value of the home. No matter what I said, they refused to believe me when I told them the market was crashing. And whenever a conversation like that ended, I knew that taking the listing would be a complete waste of my time. So I would turn down the listing. Homeowners were shocked.

On the one hand, I was still succeeding at what I was good at: I could still get appointments with sellers. On the other hand, buyers couldn't get financing to buy, home values were plunging, and the sellers were in denial. They wouldn't drop their prices to reflect the new reality. And ultimately, they paid for it. And so did I. One day, I looked up and I had worked for four straight months without a paycheck.

The net result was complete paralysis. For all intents and purposes, my team and I were shut down. Soon my stress and frustration turned to desperation. That was the beginning of almost two solid years of misery.

All of us have a natural urge to give up in the face of difficulty. It's so easy to want to give up and give in rather than staying optimistic and fighting for what you want. When something bad happens, our instinct—our "reptile brain," or whatever—tells us to curl up into a ball. It tells us to just shut ourselves down and hope the bad thing goes away.

We tell ourselves there's nothing we can do, and we collapse—*even when there are positive steps we might take to get out of that situation.*

In 2006, my "unsolvable problem" was a worldwide economic crisis. A few years later, it was a series of terrible illnesses. In all of these situations, I couldn't make the problem go away no matter how hard I worked at it. Understandably, I felt desperate and afraid. All of us deal with things like that at some point: things that stubbornly refuse to change. For some people, it's a painful episode from their past. Traumatic events and malicious people (even people who are long dead) can feel like the root cause of all our problems. I get it.

But I've also learned that you have three choices. You can curl up like a terrified reptile, paralyzed, and hope the problem will go away. (It won't.) Or you can take the opposite approach and "go all out," using the same strategy and effort to attack the problem that you've always used, knowing deep down it will no longer work. That was me for a big part of the Great Recession: working my ass off and getting appointments with sellers long after I realized it wouldn't work. Or you can turn your energy and attention to doing something else. You can take some action that gives you results, results that at the time may seem pitifully small, but that keep you headed in the right direction. Many times, the step you need to take is the one that allows you just to survive, so you can keep fighting. I'm here to assure you that when you choose the third option—the small step forward—things get better, faster. And you'll discover that you're stronger than you thought.

Ultimately, I'm convinced that the experience of trauma—something terribly difficult in your life—can help you discover strengths you didn't know you had. But first, you must actively look for a way out. You must do whatever you can to flip the situation, to exert control over it. And I'm not talking about thinking about it—I'm talking about taking action and doing something about it.

By putting this attitude into action, you learn what you're capable of. You develop some confidence. Then, when the next crisis or trauma comes, you are much better equipped to cope with it. You know you've done it before, so you have good reason to believe you can do it again. That's what I mean by renovating relentlessly.

———

Just months before the crash, I had felt like the proverbial king of the real estate world, and I lived like it. After years of struggle, starting in that garage, I was certain I had finally made it. Now—*wham*, just like that—I was watching my dream slip away. Whenever Christina and I were with her parents, my worries made it impossible for me to relax and feel comfortable. We were talking about having a family, and I was starting to think I might never be the kind of provider I wanted to be.

It was obvious that I needed to sell my "badass" house. I could no longer afford the payments. I priced it aggressively and sold it quickly to another young couple. They, in turn, found themselves in foreclosure six months later. I had sold the house to them for $1 million, and they had to sell it as a short sale for $700,000. I said goodbye to my Mercedes, my motorcycle, my BMW convertible, and, yes, my beloved Cadillac Escalade. We got Christina a Honda Civic, and I worried that we had overspent by choosing power windows instead of cheap hand-cranked ones. During the test drive, I couldn't help thinking that I had just been driving a $150,000 car, and now I was concerned about lease payments on one costing $17,000.

Knowing that I had no transportation, my dad gave me a 1994 Ford pickup truck. He had bought it off a rancher somewhere. It was a massive gray extended-cab F250. The air conditioner was broken, and there was no radio. What it did have was a hood ornament: a gigantic set of actual Texas longhorns strapped to the front grill. I would have laughed if it were someone else's—but it was mine. It was an oversized, overheated, constant reminder of my misery. Confidence is key—and I was losing my confidence. I was depressed.

Christina and I moved from one tiny apartment to the next: the first one in Placentia; the next one, a little nicer, in Newport Beach. Every day for lunch, five days a week, the two of us would go to the local Subway. We would split a five-dollar footlong, get a water cup, then "accidentally" hit the lemonade button instead of the water button. That lemonade was our splurge.

One day, I left work early. After all, what was the point? At three in the afternoon, I climbed into the ridiculous pickup, then drove—sweating all the way—to our apartment. I sat down with a Corona on the patio. That's when the old voice started playing in my head: "Maybe you aren't as good as you think. Maybe you aren't meant to be successful, and you're just like everybody else."

But I wasn't going to curl up into a ball. It was time to go into "survival mode." While we were living in Newport Beach, I started working for a local Coldwell Banker. Technically, I was still an agent, but once again I was trying anything and everything to make a living. Near our apartment was a restaurant that offered valet parking. Having always loved cars, and driving, I thought, *Why not?* I figured it would be a way to make money at night, when I finished at Coldwell Banker. So I went over there and applied for a job as a valet parker. They turned me down. They said I had no experience parking cars. I explained that I had spent two years delivering pizza all over Southern California. But they told me to get lost. Talk about rock bottom.

———

In debt, hoping to get married, and running out of options, I soon recognized that the door to a residential real estate career might be closing. I concluded that it was time to knock on a different, yet similar, door. I decided to start selling commercial real estate, with a focus on multifamily properties, because they were similar to residential housing. Commercial was the side of the industry I had always thought of as "the big boys." And it appeared to be less affected by the economic crisis.

So I got to work looking for work. From my "home office"—the kitchen table in our apartment—I started sending out résumés and making phone calls to every commercial firm I could find. Eventually, I landed interviews with the two biggest firms in Orange County. At first, both had made it clear that they weren't interested in a candidate without a college degree. So I fought to sell myself on the phone: I explained that I had attended college for two years and left for real estate sales, then very quickly became a top agent. I made sure they knew I could sell.

Both interviews were eye-opening. Both times, I found myself sitting across from management in a plush conference room, thinking, "I thought I was cocky. These guys are about the rudest, cockiest people I've ever met." My self-concept was challenged, to say the least. I couldn't help comparing myself to the people I encountered at those firms. I didn't have the education they did; I didn't have a fancy degree. But what I did have was a proven track record—which is all that should matter when it comes to sales. After all, for five years I had been successfully selling real estate. I could prove I had made serious money. And eventually, one of these "big boys" offered me a job. The offer required me to spend thousands of dollars for my own training—books and a training course—as well as a parking pass: all things I couldn't afford.

I'll never forget my first day. I arrived early, relieved to have a job and spring-loaded to get to work, to show them what I could do. The first sign that things might not go as well as I expected was when the senior agent, my team lead—to this day, perhaps the cockiest, most condescending person I have ever met—escorted me to my workstation. I won't describe it as a cubicle; that makes it sound too big. "Cubicle-esque" is more accurate. This space was tiny. And because the space was so tiny, it didn't take me long to identify its most outstanding feature: an enormous four-sided structural pillar right in the middle of it. The pillar left barely enough room for a desk and chair. And this was the only cubicle that had a pillar.

Next to this cubicle-thing was an actual cubicle: a normal, human-sized one—with no pillar. And this other cubicle was obviously vacant. So I turned to my team lead and asked, as politely as I could, "May I take the cubicle with more space?"

He barked at me: "Guys that sit *there* make six figures!"

To which I responded, "Ah. Gotcha. Well, I've been at six figures for several years now. May I have the bigger cubicle?"

"No!" he yelled, and walked off.

It was time for me to make the most of my cramped little workstation. After moving in—which didn't take long!—I went up to the front desk for my orientation with the office manager. After I introduced myself, the office manager—looking a little embarrassed—said to me, "Listen, I need to tell you something. I know your name's Tarek and everything, but I've been told we need to call you something else, and we've been thinking 'Derek.' The boss just thinks it would be more professional, or whatever. Especially around clients. So...here's your key card, Derek. Have a nice day, okay, Derek?" And he gave me my key card and another embarrassed smile as I headed, dumbfounded, back to my desk.

By the end of my first day, after I'd taken care of all the tasks I'd been given, I was more than ready to figure out how to get to the next level. I had found a way to survive; now I was ready to outperform the competition. So as everyone else left the office around 5:00 p.m., I was ready to get to work and start making phone calls.

Just as with houses, commercial listings expire when the buildings don't sell, meaning that new brokers now have the right to solicit those deals. That first night, I pulled up the MLS on my computer, just as I had done with residential listings, and found the expired multifamily listings. And I started contacting sellers. Before leaving the office at 8:00 that night, I already had several leads. The next morning, I was excited to share the news with my team lead. But to my shock—and for reasons I've never understood, to this day—he yelled at me. He was furious. Even though my calls had the potential to generate hundreds of thousands of dollars in revenue, his reaction was, *"I didn't tell you to do that!* Stop doing it! And I'm not going to call your leads!" And—once again—he stormed off.

Within a few days, I had been given a strange new assignment: to photograph every apartment building in Anaheim. That was it: to drive to Anaheim somewhere, park my car, and walk all over the place taking pictures. Since my position was entirely commission based, and this work involved no sales, no transactions of any kind, I was essentially working for free. Actually, I was spending money to work for free!

Meanwhile, I never got used to having my name changed from Tarek to Derek at that office. "Derek" never registered for me. A coworker would say, "Hey, Derek," or "Good morning, Derek," or even, "There's a call for you on line one, Derek," and I wouldn't even turn around. I was oblivious. They thought I was ignoring them. I just didn't know my own name!

It wasn't long before I'd had enough. Yes, things were still terrible for me and Christina financially. I still needed a job. And I loved commercial real estate. But I knew there had to be better options for me than working in that environment. I wasn't going to sacrifice my dignity and self-worth to the whims of an abusive boss. And I just wasn't going to answer to "Derek." Ever. A day or two later, I was gone. I loaded up a box and did the "midnight move-out." This whole experience lasted only six weeks.

———

Everywhere I looked, I saw a dead end. And I still had bills to pay. It was a miserable way to live. In a strange way, however, all of my negative self-talk motivated me. I got so angry about not making money that I was determined to prove I could.

Moreover, part of me recognized that I had been here before. Relentless renovation means that even the humblest "next right action" is better than wallowing in misery. I said to myself, "You've found success once. You can do it again." In the fall of 2007, at the lowest point in my career, I reached for my phone and called one of my original comps: Gary Lucas, the six-foot-wide real estate hero of my late teenage years. I invited him to dinner.

Christina and I met Gary one evening at an Italian place near our apartment. Trying to hide from him how much turmoil I'd been feeling, I laid everything out for him. Then I said, "Tell me what you would do."

Gary thought for a moment, then he started talking about the cold facts of the housing market. Thanks to the thousands of foreclosures, wherever you looked there was a house that was owned by, or about to be owned by, a bank. Gary said, "Tarek, imagine you're a bank. Do you really want to own that house across the street? Do you think any bank really wants to own real estate? Hell, no." Already, I was on the edge of my seat. I could tell where Gary was going. "If I were you," he said, "I'd be contacting the banks, offering to sell those houses for them."

It made perfect sense. Whenever a lender takes possession of a house it has foreclosed on, the house becomes "real estate owned," or REO. Since selling real estate is not a bank's primary business, banks typically enlist real estate agents to market and sell their REO houses for them.

By the time we stood up from the table, I had a plan. I would do everything I could to get the listings for REO properties. Thanking Gary profusely, we headed home, feeling—for the first time in a long time—hopeful.

But of course the path to success is not a straight line. When you commit to "renovate relentlessly," you understand that stuff happens: you know you'll probably have to zig and zag before you achieve success. And that's what happened.

Inspired by Gary's idea, I sat down at my computer and got busy applying to the banks to become their REO agent. Months went by and I heard nothing. As it turned out, one of the banks, Wells Fargo, responded with a yes: they sent me an email, inviting me to handle the sale of a foreclosed property—then another one, and another one after that. But I never saw any of those Wells Fargo emails, not until it was far too late. I assumed they had rejected my application without telling me. Finally—this was almost two years after I applied—I checked the spam folder of my email account. And there they were: one Wells Fargo email after another, offering me REO listings. Over the past two years, they had sent me dozens and dozens of requests to sell their properties that I never knew about. I had never responded because I hadn't seen any of the emails! In that moment, I was sick to my stomach. I was struggling and broke, and if I had just checked my spam emails two years before that, my life would have been completely different. Millions of dollars in life-changing commissions had gone straight to spam.

Fortunately, however, after months of testing the REO idea—months of twelve-hour days, testing the strategy, and failing to get any traction—I recognized that I had to pivot. I had to figure out where the real strategy was. I saw that there was opportunity for me at an earlier point in the foreclosure timeline, before the house even went to foreclosure. Just as no homeowner wants to get foreclosed on, no bank wants to have a foreclosed house on their books. That means that in many cases, a bank allows the financially distressed homeowner to sell the property in a "short sale," meaning the bank accepts less than what the borrower owes on the property. By accepting the reduced payoff, the bank crosses that troubled loan off the books. Both parties move on.

The opportunity for me, as an agent, was to get the listings as short sales before they went to the bank. I thought, if the banks don't want me to sell those listings for them, I need to get to those listings before the banks do. And I had proof that my plan would work: I had handled a successful short sale once before. So I started knocking on doors—thousands of them. I knocked on doors and cold-called thousands of distressed homeowners, hustling to represent them in short sales. Sometimes, the front door was on the other side of a big, scary dog. Even if I made it to the door safely, many times the homeowner offered to come outside and kick my ass. But I was determined to follow through with my plan. And eventually, I began to feel engaged again. I started making decent money.

All in all, that dinner with Gary was a classic "comp" encounter: not just inspirational, but educational. The idea I got from Gary didn't work out the way I expected. But it gave me hope, and it inspired me to take action. After that, I was on my own. I had to figure out the details, create a plan, and then: take massive action.

———

In the fall of 2008, our apartment complex in Newport Beach announced that rents would be going up $100 a month. With almost no money at all coming in, I knew we would have to move. Then, in November, our local news media exploded with coverage of a huge fire in the Santa Ana Canyon, not far from the Prudential office where we used to work with Brad. Hundreds of homes were damaged, and more than twenty thousand people had to be evacuated. On TV, there were reports that at the Cascades Apartments in Anaheim Hills, hundreds of units, in at least ten different buildings, had simply burned to the ground.

To Christina and me, that disaster sounded like an opportunity. Normally, we could have never afforded a two-bedroom in Anaheim Hills. But because the Cascades Apartments had been so badly damaged by the fire, we were willing to bet that no one would want to live there. Sure enough, rents had dropped to almost a thousand dollars less than what we were paying in Newport Beach. Best of all, the apartment complex was within walking distance of the Prudential Anaheim Hills office, meaning I could work with Brad Pearson again. So off to the Cascades we went.

The experience of living there was surreal. For every unit that was occupied, the next three in a row sat empty. We had no neighbors. Next door to us was an abandoned unit with charred and broken windows. After a while we got used to that. We got used to the pervasive smell of smoke and burned wood, too. But there was one thing we never did get used to. We'd be sitting in our living room, talking, when suddenly, huge flakes of ash would float by. Slowly, slowly—like giant gray feathers—these ash flakes would waft past us before settling, finally, to the floor. This phenomenon went on for months. It was eerie.

That's where Christina and I were living when we got married in April 2009. Shortly before the wedding, Christina's parents and grandparents came to visit us. As soon as they saw our apartment complex, they looked like they were going to cry. All of them were polite about it, because they knew how excited we were. But as they told us later, they were horrified by the smell of smoke and by the blackened palm trees everywhere.

The wedding itself was picture perfect: on Coronado Island, along the water, with 120 guests. Then it was back to our "hazmat-honeymoon" apartment.

———

One day in the spring of 2010, I found myself looking over some numbers. Sales prices were down 50 percent, meaning my commission checks were cut in half. There was one short sale transaction that I'll never forget. It had a first lien, a second lien, a homeowners' association lien, and an IRS lien, and it took me eleven months to negotiate the deal. After all that work, I got a check for about $7,000. Then . . . the investor I sold it to showed up, mowed the lawn, steam-cleaned the carpet, and painted the inside of the house—all of which took less than a week—and resold the house, days later, pocketing a profit of about $130,000.

Wait a minute, I thought. I did all the work here! I busted my ass! I found the seller. I found the investor. I spent a year negotiating with the bank. All to get a check for $7,000. Meanwhile, the investor did almost nothing and made about $130,000. That was the exact moment I realized I was on the wrong side of the real estate equation.

It was another one of those life-changing moments. Right then, I understood that I needed to become a real estate investor. I needed to be the person flipping these houses, buying them low and selling them high—not the one selling them cheap to investors. Which is easy to imagine when you have money—but I didn't. Nevertheless, money or no money, I knew there had to be a way.

I was confident in my real estate skills. I could see that it was all about buying a house at the right price, fixing it up, and selling it for more. All I had to do was make sure the total costs of buying, fixing, holding, and selling were less than the price I would sell it for, leaving me a profit. The less I paid for the house, the bigger my profit. That's all I knew at the time—and it was all I needed to know to get started. As for the rest, I knew I could figure it out as I went.

I started pitching my idea of house flipping to everybody I could think of, hoping to enlist them as investors. And nobody was interested. I got only two kinds of responses. One was, "Are you crazy?" I'll admit this was not a totally unreasonable response. After all, I was twenty-eight, broke, and the market was in shambles. I'm sure those people saw me as nothing more than a kid, and a broke kid at that.

The next type of response was a gentle suggestion—well-meaning, but off-target—for me to pursue a totally different business. Basically, these people came back to me with, "Tarek, instead of flipping houses, why don't you do this other thing?" For example, one friend asked me why I didn't build a luxury high-rise in downtown Los Angeles. To which I responded, "Well, for the same reason I'm not gonna put a helmet on and go play in the NFL—like, what do you think?" (As I said in Chapter Six, sometimes what you need most from your crew is mature perspective—not fantasy!)

Having every single person shut me down just made me even more determined to figure it out. The rejection was like putting fuel on my fire. No matter what it took, I was going to find someone to give me money. I had no formal business plan or fancy documents, because I didn't know how to prepare them. All I had was a piece of paper and a pen, to show the math of a real estate flip using some potential properties as examples.

Weeks went by, and my search for investors was going nowhere. Why couldn't people see what I saw? I had all of the essential information in my head—the gross, the expenses, and the net. I had a clear goal in mind, and I was certain about the path to get there. And nobody cared.

———

You may remember that when I started my real estate career I was living in my mom's garage, sleeping on a cot between a stack of paint cans and my old dirt bike. As strange as it may sound, it meant a lot to me that the dirt bike was still there. For me, it was a piece of history. When I was twelve years old, getting that dirt bike had been my ultimate dream. At twelve, I imagined myself gunning through the desert, flying over sand dunes.

In many ways, that dirt bike sums up the excitement I felt in the spring of 2010 as I thought about getting into the house-flipping business. Whenever I try to put goal setting into words, my mind goes back to that dirt bike. Getting a dirt bike had tremendous personal importance for me. That vision was crazy exciting to me, and it was very simple. Almost as soon as I dreamed about it, I took action. I grabbed some magazines and some scissors, and I cut out a bunch of photos of dirt bikes; then I planted those photos all over our house. I made it as clear to my parents as I possibly could that I wanted one. I didn't want them guessing! I had looked around for the next thing I could do that would bring me closer to my dream—in this case, cutting pictures out of magazines—and I did it. And my dream had come true. My parents bought me a dirt bike.

And that, in a nutshell, is the formula I've followed ever since. Develop that ARV of your future self: a vision that is clear, exciting, and personally fulfilling. Figure out the next step in the direction of that dream. Then go all out. Once you've taken that step, find the next one to take. Do it again, only bigger. One step at a time, go for it.

Walking out of that college lecture hall in the fall of 2003, I was determined to do whatever it took to keep getting expired listings. My goal that day was to spend the rest of my self-imposed ninety-day "testing period" doing nothing else. Every day, I had a mini-goal. It wasn't to make money. It wasn't to get listings. The only thing I focused on was making contacts: actual conversations with homeowners. To get those contacts, I knew I would have to make hundreds of phone calls a day. Meanwhile, there was no cap on the number of calls I could make. No one was going to tell me, "Stop making so many phone calls!" So I made those calls, starting at 7:45 a.m. and ending at 8:30 p.m., with a gym break in the afternoon.

Six years later, walking neighborhoods in search of potential short sales, I was determined to give it my all. I needed to work my plan like crazy, to see whether or not it was feasible. Now it was time to do the same things that had worked before, this time as an aspiring house flipper.

CHAPTER NINE

DREAM BIG

Getting into the flipping business was never my "life goal," my big dream. Frankly, before 2010, it was a business that I knew nothing about. But once I understood the numbers, I saw that it could be a big step in the right direction. I just needed a way to give it my all. I had to find out if it would work.

After striking out with one potential investor after another, I finally thought of Pete de Best, who at the time was the only person I knew who had real money. Maybe Pete would be willing to partner with me on my first house flip. I reached out to him on a Sunday afternoon, and he agreed to talk. Within seconds, Pete calmly spoke words that I'll never forget: "Yeah, if you can find a good enough deal, I'll flip a house with you," he said. "Go find it."

Pete's "Go find it" was all I needed to hear. I hadn't flipped my first house yet, but I already felt the surge of confidence you get whenever you accomplish a goal. What seemed impossible becomes real, and you find yourself looking at your next goal with an attitude of "I know I can do this."

What I learned was that you can have the best business idea in the world, but if you pitch the wrong people, they're going to shoot your idea down. I learned to beware of pitching to people who were not entrepreneurial, who weren't multimillionaires, and who didn't know any better. Soon enough, I learned to make sure the "successful people" I was pitching to were big-time successful, meaning making millions of dollars a year, versus a few hundred thousand. The takeaway: You keep asking people until you find the right people. If you don't know the right people, it sounds like you need to get out there and meet some new people!

My next step was to find a viable property for flipping. Hard work, but not impossible. Foreclosed homes in California are typically sold at an open-air auction in front of a courthouse. By Wednesday, I had found what looked like a promising property, a two-bedroom condo located on King Street in Santa Ana. The house was scheduled for auction the next day. I studied the comps—the comparable sales—and told Pete I was confident we could buy the condo with a bid of $105,000, then fix it up and make a nice profit. Pete and I agreed to meet at the courthouse steps on Thursday morning, each of us bringing cashier's checks for half that amount.

On a windy day in downtown Santa Ana, straining to hear the auctioneer as he called out the bid amounts, I listened as the bids on the condo got closer and closer to our $105,000 limit—and then went beyond it. We were about to get beaten by another bidder. Or so I thought. That's when Pete told me, "I brought extra money. Bid higher." I held up my hand and screamed, "115,000!" The auctioneer looked at me and said, "Going once—going twice—*sold*, for $115,000." In that moment, I was terrified. My hands were sweaty; my body was shaking; my heart was pounding. Part of me thought, "I'm the sucker here. No one else wanted this condo. I overpaid!" At the same time, though, I was filled with excitement, knowing I had just bought my first flip.

Pete and I had already agreed that I would manage any project that we did together, meaning I would do whatever it took to renovate the property and get it sold. So now it was time for me to take massive action on that next goal: getting the condo cleaned up, looking great, and listed for sale.

Before I could start on that, however, Christina and I had an unbreakable commitment. Mike Ferry, the real estate guru (and my favorite "professor" of the business), was about to lead a Superstar Retreat in Las Vegas. I'm always eager to hear anything that might inspire me to do more and go bigger—especially if it's coming from a comp like Mike Ferry. Meanwhile, the Great Recession was still going on, so I was especially open to new ideas. So—maxing out our credit cards—off to Las Vegas we went.

On the first day, Mike Ferry established his basic message: When you have the right mindset, anything is possible. Mike challenged everyone in the audience to act on that mindset in a very specific way. For one night, Mike instructed us—all five thousand of us—to live the life that we always dreamed of. Our "homework" was to simply live the life that we wanted, beginning that same afternoon. He told us to buy clothes we couldn't afford, then go out for a dinner we couldn't afford, and drink wine we couldn't afford. And that's what we did. For one night, we lived life at the next level. I took Christina shopping. We bought the nicest clothes we had ever owned. Christina bought a gorgeous black and gold dress with shoes to match. I bought a Zegna suit that was 60 percent off, marked down to $800. I was so proud. That night, we went out to dinner at the fanciest restaurant we could find, an Italian place in the New York–New York Casino. We treated ourselves to top-shelf champagne, which would normally be way beyond our budget, and multiple courses of fine Italian cuisine. For that one night, we didn't worry about the cost. We just talked about the future and our goals; we agreed that everything was going to work itself out. To this day, it's one of the most memorable days of my life—in spite of my physical condition the next day.

"Renovating relentlessly" means that you show up, no matter what. No matter how much you celebrate or how late you stay up, you still show up in the morning. It's an essential part of taking massive action. You live with the consequences of your actions! And when we arrived at the ballroom for Day Two the next morning, my head was pounding, I was dizzy, and I worried I might throw up. Christina and I found seats in a dark corner at the back of the room. Meanwhile, I could see the "superstars"—the heads of real estate companies and other VIP guests—taking their seats in the front row. One of them was Brad Pearson. Shortly after the session began, a VIP couple sitting next to Brad had to leave the event. Brad texted me and invited Christina and me to come up and take the empty seats. As awful as I felt, I told myself to suck it up. I nudged Christina and said, "Let's do it."

When we got to the front and slid into our "superstar" seats, Mike Ferry was already in full swing onstage. But as soon as I lifted my head to look at Mike, the room started spinning. Sweat began dripping down my forehead, and my heart was thumping in my chest. I thought I might be having a heart attack. One of the attendees came running across the front row to me. Disregarding what was happening onstage, he knelt beside me and said, "Buddy, you don't look so good." He handed me a bottle of water and some Advils, then went back to his seat.

By the time of the midmorning break, I was feeling a lot better. Because of where we were sitting, Christina and I were surrounded by the people we had seen speaking onstage for years. We found ourselves chatting with our real estate heroes. One of them asked, "Hey, who are you guys? We haven't seen you up here before." I suppressed the urge to say, "We're nobodies—we're freaking peons!" But that's what I was thinking. Then a blond, sharply dressed, youthful-looking guy with a dazzling smile came over. It was the guy who had rescued me with Advils and water. Now that I was able to focus, I realized who he was: Chad Vidmark, the guy who was onstage the day before, talking about how he made $800,000 per year. He was a VIP from Palm Springs who had shared the speaker's platform with Mike Ferry the day before. Clearly, Chad had found huge success in real estate. It turned out that my Good Samaritan was a superstar broker! And as casually as I could, I said, "So, Chad—what do you do to get business?"

"Well," he said, "I have a local TV show in Palm Springs. I use it to showcase my listings on the weekends. Thanks to that little show, everybody in the area knows who I am. You'd be amazed. It's like I'm a local celebrity."

"Interesting," I said. "What does that do, exactly?"

And Chad said, "Well, people recognize me, and then they want to work with me."

I remember thinking, *Great idea*, but in that moment, the idea of a TV show was too big to comprehend. It took me a while to appreciate the possibilities. A couple of nights later, back home, I was sitting on the couch at about ten o'clock, and—as usual—a thousand ideas were bouncing around in my head. This one suddenly crystallized. All the "comp" elements were there, instantly. My Vegas chat with a real estate superstar—someone I admired and wanted to emulate—was suddenly pointing me toward a concrete "how-to," a doable step that I was more than ready to take. True, I knew nothing about being on TV. But I saw that Chad Vidmark was doing it, so I knew it could be done. *A TV show.* Maybe there was a way for me not just to emulate what Chad was doing, but to enhance it. I would give it my all. Either it would work or it wouldn't.

It's still a vivid memory. Christina walked past me on her way upstairs to bed. She put one foot on the bottom step, turned to me, and asked, "Hey, are you coming to bed?"

"No," I said. "I'm going to get us a TV show."

It came out of my mouth just like that: completely out of the blue. It must have sounded absurd. Christina laughed.

"Okay…" she said. "And what are we going to get a TV show *about?*"

I paused. The details were still taking shape in my mind. Once I found the words, they were life changing.

"Well, we just bought our first flip," I said. "What if we flip houses on TV? We'll call it—I don't know—*Flip or Flop*. Flip, if we make it, or flop if we go bust." Little did I know that this jokey idea would become the name of a hit TV show that would last ten years.

Christina laughed again, called me crazy, and headed upstairs to bed.

That night, I stayed up late. I grabbed my laptop and Googled "Hollywood production companies." I came across one whose website had a button labeled "Casting." That button opened to a page that said, "Send us pictures, and tell us about your show idea."

I got busy writing a description of what I wanted our flipping show to be. Then I pulled together some photos. I checked and rechecked all of it, making sure it was as good as I could make it. Then I hit "Send."

———

For me, the first stage of any new project, the learning stage, is often painfully difficult. I absorb as much information as I can, but until the project actually "takes off," I get frustrated by my lack of progress, or what feels to me like a lack of progress. Then, once I see evidence that the new activity is working, I tend to get so excited that I forget how difficult the learning stage was.

For example, I've been in real estate long enough to have forgotten—*almost* forgotten!—how painful those training classes were at Wise Ol' Owl. That particular "learning stage" did not come naturally to me at all. But I had to get it done. Likewise, getting back into the gym, with Justin, was awful, but for a slightly different reason. I already knew what to do; I knew all about sets and reps and making my way around the gym. What was new for me, and what I needed to learn, was getting past my embarrassment about looking so sloppy and fat. Once I started to see results, that was all I needed for my exercise routine to catch fire; I became passionate about working out. I guess you could say that I'm all about the "implementing" phase. Once I know what to do, stand back, because I'm going all out. It's the phase before that, the learning phase, that is tough for me.

The reality is that you can't skip the learning phase. When I started flipping, all I knew was that I could make a lot more money flipping than I could doing short sales. I still had a lot to learn about the "how" of flipping. And, of course, I knew absolutely nothing about being on TV.

In hindsight, learning those things was the easy part. I never could have imagined how difficult the next few years were going to be, and how much I would have to learn—and relearn—about life. Off the set, and away from the lights and TV cameras, I was about to begin some of the worst years of my life. Those years "reeducated" me in some of the flip-your-life fundamentals that I've already shared with you here. I had to go back to basics.

For starters, I was reminded that you don't fully appreciate the good times until you've experienced the bad times. As I've said, even the most painful episodes in your life can be a gift: they make you stronger; they thicken your skin and set you up for even greater success. But I also learned, all over again, that when the bad times come, you need to have a crew of people who support and encourage you. You need to be able to ask for help. Above all, there are times in your life when you need to tell yourself, *Just take the next step.*

———

The morning after hitting "Send" with my proposal, I heard back from the production company. They said, in so many words, "Hey, we liked your look, and we like what you're doing. Send us a home video."

In other words, in the space of a week or so in the summer of 2010, Christina and I had our first fixer-upper; I had enlisted Pete de Best as our investor; and—with the thumbs-up we got from the production company to submit a video—we had at least a chance of getting "a little TV show" of our own. The best news of all: Christina was now about five months pregnant.

My first challenge was that the production company wanted a video, and at that point our list of completed projects totaled zero. That meant that the King Street condo, our one and only property, was the perfect candidate!

My next challenge was that we didn't have a video camera, and we couldn't afford one. Then I thought of Brad Pearson, our manager at Prudential. Among his other interests, Brad was an "electronics nerd" who loved any kind of gadget. I called Brad to see if he had a video camera I could borrow. When he said yes, I drove to the office to pick it up.

"I want to flip houses on TV—like, a TV show," I explained. "I'm gonna call it *Flip or Flop*. Other people I've told about the idea think I'm crazy. What do you think?"

And Brad said, "I think you're insane, Tarek. But I also think it's the best damn idea you've ever had. I would watch that show."

Carefully placing his camera in my hands, Brad gave me a little tutorial on how to use it. As I headed out the door with his gear, he said, "Dude, don't break my camera. It's new." Brad knew me all too well.

———

To save money, I was planning on playing general contractor and doing as much of the work on King Street as I could by myself. And whenever there was work going on, I tried to film it. Most of the time I just had the camera sitting on a bucket, or against the wall, filming my best attempt at manual labor. The whole thing quickly became a comedy of errors. I had a lot to learn.

Once we had the new flooring down, it was time to put the baseboards back in place. But before that happened, they needed to be painted. I got into an argument with the painter, and I fired him. Then I figured, *How hard can painting be?* So I bought a drop cloth, spread it out on the living room floor, set the baseboards out on it, and started painting. As I painted, I was filled with pride: *Sure enough*—I thought—*you can do this!* When I finished, and the baseboards were dry, I reached to pick them up. That's when I discovered that I had a problem. Somehow, the paint had seeped through the drop cloth, straight onto the brand-new floor. Now that they were dry, the baseboards were stuck to the drop cloth, and the drop cloth was stuck to the floor. I was furious. I spent the next four hours on my hands and knees, scrubbing the paint off the new living room floor.

Next came the new bathroom vanity light. I was hard at work remodeling the bathroom when Christina stopped by. She got excited when she saw the new fixture, and she asked me to hold it up, to see how it would look once it was installed. I held the thing up where the light would go—not realizing there were live wires there. The next thing I knew, my teeth were tightly clenched, my whole body was buzzing, and the light fixture was sparking. I was sure I was being electrocuted. I'm surprised the video didn't show smoke coming out of my ears.

Once that fun was over, it was time to acid-wash the shower tile. The acid-washing kit came with some scary safety instructions, so I made sure I followed them. I put on the rubber gloves, kicked my sandals off, and stepped into the shower. I poured some acid on the special sponge and got to work, scrubbing the walls like the Karate Kid: acid on, acid off. I was feeling extremely proud. After a few minutes of scrubbing the shower walls, I began to feel an odd tingling around the edges of my feet. In a nanosecond, the tingle rocketed to a Level 10, Code Red, nuclear assault on every inch of my feet. They might as well have been on fire.

Screaming, I jumped out of the shower and into the bathtub. I fumbled with the faucet. *Squeak-squeak-squeak*: no water. I remembered that the new owner—meaning me—had turned off all the water to the condo. Still screaming, I dashed out of the bathroom, out the front door of the condo, straight to the community pool, and jumped in.

We got almost all of this on video. Then I took the camera back to Brad—dented, badly scratched, and splattered with paint. Brad looked horrified. I explained that we had given the project everything we had, and the camera suffered. We dropped it. We cracked it. And I had no money to buy Brad a new one.

Meanwhile, we had shot tons of video, and I had no clue what to do with it. So—testing Brad's friendship even further—I handed him the memory chip and his broken camera and asked for another favor: "Brad, can you make this footage into a finished video for the production company? 'Cause I have no idea how to do it."

And very, very fortunately, Brad came through again. First, of course, he gave me grief about his camera. But then he said, "Yeah, I'll make a video for you." Over the next four days, editing the video on his home computer, Brad condensed those hours of footage into thirty-eight minutes. His edits captured the essence of what we had done with the condo, including the disasters. Ultimately, thanks to Brad's camera, his creativity, and his willingness to help, I had a video that was lively and funny and communicated everything that Christina and I had hoped for. Thanking Brad profusely, we sent the video off to the production company.

———

To our delight, our very first flip, the King Street condo, sold very fast. I had completed all the renovations, start to finish, in fifteen days. Forty-eight hours later, we had it listed for sale. A few days after listing it, we found a buyer at full price, and thirty days later, we closed on the sale. Christina, Pete, and I realized a profit of around $34,000, close to a 30 percent return in under sixty days—certainly enough to keep all three of us motivated. A couple of months after that, we were working on two more flips. The business was moving ahead.

Before long, we got some more exciting news. The production company liked our video enough to follow up with a sizzle reel: their own, professionally produced overview of what the TV show could be. The sizzle would be a more sophisticated sample they would send to the networks, in hopes of getting a series. *Holy crap!* I thought. *This is getting real!*

At dawn on our first day of filming, a five-person crew showed up at our house, fixed us up with tiny clip-on microphones, and told us they would be following us around for the day—from 7:00 a.m. to 5:00 p.m. They wanted us to do what we normally did. I had already gone out and scouted a couple of homes that were up for auction that day. The crew was filming us when we went online that morning and pulled up the listings, to make sure the houses we'd targeted were still up for auction. We ran the comparable sales to come up with a value and went to the bank to get some cashier's checks. Then it was off to the auction, with a producer riding shotgun and a cameraman in the back. We did our best to stay cool and composed on camera, but it was July in Southern California, and the temperature was close to 100. I've never loved the heat, but I wasn't the one who was pregnant. Christina was miserably uncomfortable.

Meanwhile, we had stiff competition for the property we wanted, including one guy who appeared at every auction. In his stained fishing hat and rumpled clothes, this guy could have passed as homeless. But we had learned that he was the biggest buyer at any auction. He always had millions of dollars in cashier's checks stashed in his fanny pack. We hung in there in the bidding and hoped it would be enough, especially with the crew following our every move, but in the end the guy with the fanny pack outbid us. We tried to take it in stride, keeping in mind that the production company crew had told us to do what we would normally do. From there, we drove to one of our flips to check on it as the production crew followed us around. Back home, still being filmed, we played an intense round of Nintendo Wii bowling, then sat for some final questions on camera. And that was that.

Over the next couple of months, the production company called us in for more interviews. We were happy to oblige. I'll never forget arriving for our first meeting. The company's building is in North Hollywood, one of the densest, busiest areas in the country. Sure enough, their parking lot had zero spaces available. For a moment, I thought we'd have to park three miles away to get to this meeting. I had flashbacks of being that miserable college kid, waiting in line to get a spot. I remembered how angry and lost I had always felt in those college parking lots. Then, as we turned down the last row, there in a parking space sat two orange cones. Taped to the cones was a little white piece of paper, flapping in the wind. And written on the paper was "El Moussa—Tarek and Christina." We didn't have a show yet, but it already felt that way. "We have a parking spot!" I shouted, as amazed as a kid on Christmas Day.

After that, everything was in the production company's hands. They prepared to present us to the networks. And the wait began.

———

Months later, we still hadn't heard anything, and the production company said it wasn't looking good. I swallowed my disappointment, telling myself, "At least you gave it a shot." And I moved on. Stuff happens, and you have to pivot; you have to focus on the next goal.

We had more than enough to keep us occupied. That fall of 2010, we welcomed our firstborn, a precious little girl with big green eyes and a wisp of strawberry-blonde hair. We named her Taylor. Four ecstatic grandparents were now coming in and out of our house, and Christina and I learned what a rock star you become when you bring a grandchild into the world. Now Christina focused more on being a mom, while I stayed on the hunt for flips.

HGTV!

In June 2011, eleven months after the taping of our sizzle reel, I was on the golf course and about to tee off when my cellphone rang. It was the production company.

"Tarek, you're not gonna believe this. HGTV wants to do a pilot!"

All I could think to say was, "Whaaat?" This was huge! I knew the production company had sent our sizzle reel to thirteen different networks. But HGTV was the one that Christina and I wanted the most. HGTV was dynamic and established and perfect for us. I called Christina to celebrate. We couldn't believe it. It was actually happening.

As soon as we received the contract for the pilot, my first move was to ask an attorney to review it. The contract was packed with legalese, and this review couldn't wait. Nothing on the project could go forward until it was signed. A friend recommended an entertainment lawyer named Roger Behle (sounds like "Bailey"), so I reached out to Roger and asked him to look at the contract. Roger told me, "I'd love to," and he gave us an estimate of what it would cost, which wasn't an amount that seemed crazy or unfair. It just happened to be money we didn't have.

"I can't come up with the money right now," I told Roger, "but we've got a couple of deals closing soon. Can we just pay later?" Roger laughed and said, "No problem."

Since that first conversation, Roger has become my voice of reason, a trusted counselor, a mentor, and one of my best friends. We still laugh about it to this day. *Pay later?* Attorneys rarely work on an "installment plan." Had it been anyone else, the odds are that I would have been given a polite version of "No way in hell!"—if I had heard back at all. But Roger was different. He was referred by my "crew."

"No sweat, we'll make it work," he said. "Happy to help you, and I understand the time constraints you are under."

What can I say? We lucked out big time. Since that first contract, Roger has negotiated millions of dollars in deals for me. I was lucky to be able to enlist him as a member of my "crew."

———

That summer of 2011, we filmed the pilot, which was our third-ever flip. The production company warned us that the odds of getting a show were low, and that we should expect to wait for up to a year to find out. There were no guarantees.

Defying expectations, within weeks of finishing the pilot episode, we heard from HGTV. They were offering us a contract for thirteen thirty-minute episodes on national TV. *Flip or Flop* was on its way to making it on air! Our first reaction was: *Amazing!*

Our second reaction was: *Wait a second. So far, we have flipped three houses, total.* The HGTV contract required us to do thirteen houses, in ten months, on television. "How in the heck are we going to do so many houses?" Christina asked. "Where are we going to find the money?" She put into words what I was already thinking. Problem One: We didn't have the money to buy that many houses. Problem Two: Houses that are suitable for flipping can be very hard to find; it takes time to find even one. Even if we had the money, we didn't know how to find that many houses in such a short time frame. We still didn't really know how to flip houses!

While I was mulling that over, I asked Roger Behle to look at the contract. As we talked, I asked him to give me the worst-case scenario. If, for some reason, we couldn't fulfill all of HGTV's expectations, what could happen?

Roger was blunt. "Well," he said, "the network could sue you. The worst case is that the two of you end up losing everything you own."

I looked around our crummy apartment. We owned almost nothing. The few things we had weren't worth very much.

"You know what?" I said. "If things don't work out, they can have it—all of it!"

As tough as our contractual commitment was, we weren't about to back off. (Because… "dirt bike. Duh!") So when Christina asked, "How are we going to do this?" there could be only one answer.

"I don't know," I said. "We'll find a way."

Suddenly, we needed to learn how to be on television. And it's probably fair to say that, in those early days, the production company and the network people were learning right alongside us. After all, *Flip or Flop* was one of the first flipping shows on TV, which seems almost hard to believe now, given the explosion of similar shows. In late 2011 and early 2012, all of us—HGTV, the production company, and Christina and I—were trying to figure it out as we went.

Producing a show like *Flip or Flop* requires juggling two very different schedules: the TV production schedule and the construction schedule. In the early days of the show, the two schedules were completely out of sync. The TV people would get the footage they needed for one episode, then they'd say, "We're ready to do another house!" But there wasn't another house yet. They would ask, "Where's the next house?" And I would have to admit, "I haven't bought it yet!" Then I would jump into action and figure it out.

Fortunately, finding the money wasn't the issue. That part was challenging, but not impossible. Pete de Best, my investor-turned-business-partner, started funding more deals, and together, we went out and raised more money. The much bigger challenge was finding houses fast enough to satisfy the production schedule. I still had my "day job" as an agent at Prudential Anaheim Hills; I was still selling real estate. But now I took on two entirely different roles: in addition to being a conventional agent, I was a buyer—an investor—and a TV personality! I had to do whatever it took to find that next house, and the next one, and the one after that. And I had to flip those houses on TV, which made the process exponentially more difficult.

Typically, the addresses of foreclosure properties are announced the night before an auction. But I knew I couldn't bid on just any house. I needed to go see them. And it wasn't just about making sure they were viable flips. We couldn't film the show at any house that people were still living in. I had to make certain that the houses were vacant. So at least three nights a week, after getting home from the office at 8:30 or 9:00, eating dinner, and studying the listings for the next day's auctions, I would open up MapQuest and plan a route to, say, twenty homes in different cities throughout Southern California. By 10:00 p.m., leaving Christina to take care of Taylor, I'd be in my car, starting my loop of those twenty homes. At each one, I'd be looking for telltale signs: Were there cars in the driveway? Was the grass overgrown? Were newspapers and trash piling up? Were the window shades gone, or were the windows boarded up? Many times, I just had to go with my best guess as to whether anyone still lived there.

I was driving all over Southern California again, but this time with a mission and a purpose. I would hit all the four major counties, and I would usually get home around 4:00 in the morning, after spending six hours on the road. And no matter how things turned out—no matter long I was out the night before, scouting houses—I was at work and going full speed at Prudential by 8:00 the next morning.

And if I found possible flips in my nighttime searches, that didn't mean my problem was solved. Even when the homes looked decent enough for me to bid on, the actual auctions were always challenging. Out of twenty good candidates for flips, inevitably only four or five would actually be auctioned; the others would show up on the auction schedule as "postponed—postponed—postponed." Meanwhile, there was no way I could compete with the "big boys," the buyers with plenty of cash. Time and time again, I was outbid. Finally, at one auction, at the end of the day, after almost everyone had left, the property I wanted was announced. I bid, nobody bid against me, and I got the house. I couldn't believe I got it. They should have bid against me, but they didn't. I learned that if I keep showing up, every now and then I'm going to get lucky.

Real estate investors know that as soon as you buy a house to flip, you've got to move quickly to convert it and sell it. In a very real sense, time is money in the flipping business, and if the house is just sitting there idle, it gets very expensive. It's expensive because flip houses typically have hard-money loans with interest rates above 8 percent. That means you're making a high-interest mortgage payment on an empty house. Every second of every day, there's a cost. When you're sleeping, you are paying for that house, and your investment isn't making any money. But now that the TV show was underway, we couldn't work on the house unless the cameras were there, so it slowed things down, which meant I had a lot more carrying costs. For example, I would see that the bathroom needed retiling, but I couldn't start until the camera crew arrived. Sometimes, the crew didn't arrive for three days, so I was losing money. For a while, the two schedules just never seemed to line up. HGTV and the production company kept asking us for more flips, faster. The result was that houses I expected to finish in three months were taking six months to finish. Meanwhile, I was thinking, *This is crazy! We're drowning in costs!*

Time to ask for help. Just as I had asked Gary Lucas for help, at an earlier moment of exhaustion and stress, now I reached out to our new "entertainment guru," Roger Behle, and asked him for advice. Roger helped us figure out how to become efficient. We saw that by "blocking out" five or six houses in production at once, we could "leapfrog" the TV activity from one house to another. Once filming was finished at one house, we could shuttle to the next house, and the next one, without stopping production. By trial and error, we—meaning the production company, HGTV, and Christina and I—got better and better at juggling project houses this way. But this process, and the mechanics of financing all of it, were things we had to learn, and learning it took a long time.

———

Shows like *Flip or Flop* are filmed up to a year before they air, so for all of 2012 and the first part of 2013, we had no idea if any of this was even working. In fact, halfway into the filming for our first season of *Flip or Flop*, production was completely shut down. It stopped cold. Eventually, we learned that while most of the folks at HGTV loved what we were doing, there was one doubter. A higher-up at the network worried that our show might not be consistent with the network's brand. Everything stood still while "the powers that be" debated the show's future. In the end, we were able to move forward, and from 11:00 p.m. until 12:00 midnight, with no promotion or marketing at all, on April 16, 2013, the first two episodes of *Flip or Flop* aired back-to-back. We celebrated with a watch party at a restaurant in Los Angeles with our production team and family. We rented a limo and took our parents in style. It was a night we'll never forget. We had given this new opportunity everything we had. Now it was time to see if it worked.

As the opening credits came up, I was thrilled, and I was terrified. It was a surreal experience to see ourselves on the big screen. Since there had been no promotion for the show—no coordinated wave of commercials or marketing—I worried that no one would even know to watch. But... something special happened. Over the course of the hour—between

11:00 and midnight—our viewership jumped 43 percent. The next day, we learned that our little unknown show was one of the top hundred most-watched shows that day, across all of television. Making the top hundred shows in the Nielsen ratings, with our first show out of the gate, surprised everyone; it was mind-blowing. Two weeks later, HGTV changed our time slot to prime time: Thursday nights at 9:00 p.m. Before long, the show was outperforming any show on cable on Thursdays, and on many Thursday nights, we were #1 on TV. It was obvious that people wanted to watch. We were off and running with our new TV career. I couldn't believe it, but it worked.

CHAPTER TEN

REMEMBER THE BASICS

If you were to ask me why I thought *Flip or Flop* took off as it did, I would say it was because our fans loved that we were regular people just like them. They could see that we were a young family putting everything on the line. That first year, we were half-broke most of the time. But we kept at it. We quickly learned that our viewers cared about us as people. To our amazement, our little "crew" was growing into a worldwide audience.

The tremendous value of the relationship with my audience came home to me in a dramatic way in the spring of 2013. As I say, life has a way of teaching you lessons, sometimes harsh ones, that force you back to the basics.

———

The first season of *Flip or Flop* had just premiered on HGTV, and we were weeks into filming our second season. A viewer out of Texas named Ryan

Reade was watching the show when she noticed a suspicious lump on my neck. Very fortunately for me, Ryan was a registered nurse, and she took the initiative to email our producers to express her concern. I had been vaguely aware, before this, that something was going on, because I found myself constantly clearing my throat. I had even visited a general practitioner, multiple times, about my throat-clearing. But the GP had simply given me a prescription for Flonase, a nasal spray for allergies. In reality, my thyroid gland had become so enlarged that it was putting pressure on my windpipe.

Ryan's email set off alarm bells. Clearly, something was wrong, and I knew I needed an expert opinion from a different doctor. I requested an ultrasound. It came back inconclusive. But a biopsy done at the same time came back as "atypical," meaning something either could, or could not, be seriously wrong. Meanwhile, I learned that thyroid cancer most often shows up as just a lump in the neck, and that blood screens and other tests are often normal; it's not unusual for the patient to feel fine. So my doctor recommended exploratory surgery. In my case, at least, surgery was the only way to figure out what was really happening with me.

What was supposed to be a one-hour procedure to take a look at the lump became, instead, over four hours on the operating table. I'll never forget the moment I found out why it had taken so long. I was just coming to, in the recovery room, when I opened my eyes and saw Christina looking down at me, bawling. Tears were running down her face.

It took every bit of energy I had to ask her the question. "I have cancer, don't I?"

"Yes," she sobbed. And that was a life-changing moment.

Going into the surgery, I didn't think I had cancer. When I woke up, I learned that I had Stage 3 thyroid cancer, meaning it had spread to the lymph nodes in my neck. Not only had the surgeon completely removed my thyroid, but he had also taken out all the nearby lymph nodes.

It was one of those moments when I felt like I was living in a nightmare. My mind raced as I searched for anything positive, anything at all that I could cling to.

As it turned out, Christina and I had just found out that her cousin, who is roughly the same age as I am, had also developed cancer, which in his case was testicular cancer. So I tried to make light of my negative situation.

"At least I don't have that one!" I said.

But of course I was devastated. I felt an instant and almost overwhelming terror for myself. Even worse, though, were my fears for my little family, and the knowledge that our precious two-year-old, Taylor, might lose her dad. Before I left the hospital, I had been given a plan: there would be regular follow-ups to review my progress, and at the first of these appointments, my oncologist would tell me about the next recommended phase of treatment—radioactive iodine therapy.

The terrible discovery of my thyroid cancer prompted me and Christina to dig into my old medical records. I discovered that in 2012, a routine testicle exam had been noted as "irregular." But nothing else was said, and no referrals were made. At my first post-op appointment, while I was scheduling the radioactive iodine treatment, I mentioned this to my oncologist. He immediately called the imaging center, which was in the same medical complex, to schedule an ultrasound exam. By chance, a time slot had just opened up. So over to imaging I went.

I changed into a hospital gown, climbed onto the table, and started making small talk with the ultrasound tech as he did his thing, passing the wand over me and occasionally glancing at his monitor. It helped that the tech was a talkative guy, because I was in an uncomfortable situation. We chatted about surfing and other sports, and for the first few minutes everything went fine.

Then—I will never forget this—this chatty technician went completely silent. He was staring at his monitor, and his facial expression seemed off. I got up on my elbows and said to him, "Dude—*what is it?*"

The tech looked at me with a startled expression.

"I'm not a doctor," he said. "I can't say anything."

"You're seeing something," I insisted. "What is it?"

Again, he said, "I'm not a doctor." But then he asked, "Are you in pain?"

His question confused me. I couldn't tell what he was trying to get at. Then he said, "If you're in pain, the emergency room is down the hall." That was the exact moment I knew I was in trouble. It was clear that he was pointing me toward the emergency room for a reason. So down the hall I went.

Twenty minutes later, an ER doctor confirmed what had been obvious to the tech, and just like that, I found out I had testicular cancer.

———

As heavyweight boxer Mike Tyson once famously said, "Everybody has a plan until they get punched in the mouth." I was still only thirty-one, and I now had two types of cancer. It was beyond my ability to take it all in. I didn't know much about cancer to begin with. Frankly, almost nobody in my age group even talked about it much. Now all I could think was, *There is no possible way this can be happening.* How could I be thirty-one years old and have two different cancers? Especially two that were so far apart in my body?

After doing everything I could to hold it all in, I finally broke down. *Shit, I'm going to die,* I thought, and the tears flowed. The shock was overwhelming. All I could say to Christina was, "*This is it.*"

Only weeks earlier it had been a bad joke, my attempt at humor, about how it could always be worse; at least I wasn't losing a testicle. Now, ironically, it turned out I did have to have a testicle removed. Christina and I had talked about having another child. I was sure this meant no more kids for us. I was reeling. Before I left the ER, I was put on a schedule for surgery to remove the testicle. All in all, the "plan" I'd had when I'd left home earlier that day was in pieces.

———

Going back to basics means refusing to dwell on negative information. It means staring your problems in the face and confronting them head-on. It *doesn't* mean adding new layers of anxiety to what is already awful. As hard as it is, you do everything you can to find the positive within the negative. You ask for help. You reach out to other people. And you accept what you can't change, so that you can focus your precious energy on things you can change. Once you know what you can change, it's time to do something, to take action. Thinking about changing isn't going to change anything; you have to act. You have to throw yourself into whatever will bring results.

And at that moment, what I hoped would bring results was the next phase of treatment, which involved a weeklong quarantine to minimize everyone else's exposure to the radioactivity from my body. While my lymph nodes were bombarded with radioactive iodine, my "home" was a pleasant-enough hospital room with a full bathroom and shower, a couch, and a little sitting area—it was like being locked up in a little hotel room. On the first day, a hospital staffer in personal protective equipment, or PPE, including a face shield and mask, led me in, handed me a large metal pill, and asked me to swallow it. When she left, locking the door behind her, it dawned on me that I was now in solitary confinement. From time to time during that week, I'd be sitting on the couch, and someone would slide my lunch tray through a slot in the door. At other times, there would be a knock on the door, and a warning voice would say, "I'm coming in to take a reading. Please stand on the opposite side of the room." Then someone in full PPE would come in, armed with what looked like a laser gun, to check my radioactivity level. They would point this gun at me as if I were a target. Then they would nod goodbye and disappear. It was terribly lonely.

Considering my medical problems, both the production company and the network, HGTV, had already hinted that it might be the end of *Flip or Flop*. They were certainly gracious about it; they expressed deep sympathy for my situation and told me how sorry they were to hear my terrible news. The gist of it was, "We imagine you need to focus all of your energy and attention on your physical health, and we certainly understand, and it's probably time to shut down the show."

Alone and fearful, and desperate to stop thinking about my health, that was exactly where I was focusing my energy and attention: on the show and on the business. I thought about the promise of *Flip or Flop*, and all the wonderful things that could come into our lives because of it. I thought about the fact that, with one season behind us, we had already established a solid brand and had a devoted audience.

So the next time the TV people gently suggested shutting down the show, my response was firm: "Thank you, but no thank you. We're not shutting anything down." I made it clear that nothing was over, and I was going to do whatever it took to film Season 2 of *Flip or Flop*.

I might have been in solitary confinement, but I was determined to keep working. The challenge was that as soon as I swallowed that metal pill, anything I touched turned radioactive. So I ordered a brand-new laptop, a "burner" cellphone, and a headset, knowing that I would have to throw them away when I left, since they would be unsafe for anyone to use. Thanks to my makeshift "office," whenever I wasn't getting medical treatment I stayed in close contact with Christina, my employees, and the production team. To the best of my ability, I kept going.

When the week ended and I was released from quarantine, I dropped every bit of my technical gear into the trash can. I left behind the brand-new computer, the headset, and the phone—everything. I was reminded of walking out of that college geology class years before, intentionally abandoning my stuff. Only this time, every bit of my stuff was radioactive.

I was warned not to go within six feet of Christina or our baby for two full weeks. Anything I touched would become radioactive. And that, by far, was the hardest part of the whole ordeal: worrying about keeping a safe distance from my family. I was too scared to risk being anywhere near them, so I decided, *Screw that. I'm not even going home!*

We had just bought a flip house in Barstow, California, almost halfway from Los Angeles to Las Vegas. It was the farthest away that we had ever purchased a house. I climbed into my truck and made a quick call to Christina to tell her not to expect me. Then I headed out of the hospital parking lot, without a thought in my head of what the big picture might be, or what the next days and weeks might look like. I just drove to Barstow. Once I got there, and I had poked around the flip house for a little while, I figured I would spend the night at a local motel. But as soon as I got back in my truck, I started thinking about the people who would occupy my motel room after I left. Wasn't I putting them at risk of exposure to radioactivity?

Back to basics. To this day, I am thankful for my firefighter friend, Ronnie Skyberg—fellow survivor of the "Newport nightmare"—for taking me in. Just minutes after I called him, Ronnie said, very simply, "Come on over." He assured me that he didn't care about his potential exposure to radioactivity. It was that simple, and it was a huge relief: "Come on over."

And for the next two weeks, from the couch in Ronnie's living room, I kept things going, checking in with Christina and my team. I did everything I could to stay connected with my family, my businesses, home sales, new developments—the things that for almost fifteen years had given me meaning and purpose.

———

Losing your entire thyroid gland does a number on you. Because your thyroid hormones affect so many other systems in the body, completely losing that little "hormone factory" will affect your weight, your energy, and your mood—to name just a few. The T3 and T4 hormones that used to be produced naturally must now be supplied synthetically, which in turn becomes a balancing act. Not enough hormone, and you're prone to being anxious, depressed, and extremely tired: it feels like you're walking around in a daze. Too much hormone, and your mind races: you're prone to having an elevated heartbeat, high blood pressure, and extreme irritability; you can't concentrate; and you have trouble sleeping. Your emotional baseline starts at a "9," because you're already living with anxiety; the slightest thing will move you to a "10."

Sure enough, the months after my surgeries were a roller-coaster ride. For starters, in order to get ready for my radioactive iodine treatment, I was put on a diet that eliminated all iodine, and I had to stop taking any and all medications. Meanwhile, now that my thyroid was gone, my weight ballooned; I gained fifty pounds almost overnight. Back on the set of our TV show, filming continued, but I was miserable all the time. I was terribly nauseous and developed migraine headaches, again because I had no more T3 or T4 hormones, at all, while I was waiting for my radioactive iodine treatment. From time to time, I'd have to stop filming and excuse myself to go throw up. Worst of all, my energy was completely gone. Normally, from the second I wake up, I'm going full throttle; now I was already spent before the day even began. But even though I felt wiped out, I was determined to fight through this cancer and all of its consequences. I had decided that I would not slow down. I refused to quit. Whatever was within my control, I would control. And we kept going.

———

Sometimes, the "massive action" you need to take is as basic as putting one foot in front of the other. In those moments, the most important step in your life is the next one.

Less than nine months after finishing my cancer treatment, I felt good enough to play some golf. The anxiety, brain fog, and fatigue had not gone away, but I wanted the distraction of spending a few hours outdoors in the sunshine doing something I enjoyed.

I was finishing one of the last holes of the course when I felt a spasm in my back. Something was obviously wrong, because there was continuous pain. In hindsight, I should have stopped playing immediately. But I'm the type of person who tries to fight through things. Plus, I was having a record round—literally, the best round of my life—so I kept going.

At the next tee, I set up for my drive and started my swing. As I came down to swing through, suddenly I was on the ground, seized by the worst pain I've ever felt in my life. My entire lower back and legs seemed to be on fire. The pain radiated across and down my back, down my butt and legs, all the way to my toes. My friends helped me into the golf cart and got me to my car. Somehow I drove myself to the nearest hospital, but when I pulled up in front of the emergency room, opened my car door, and tried to get out, I dropped to the pavement. I started crawling to the door. Nurses came running. All I could say was, "Please help me."

That was the beginning of fifteen months of a whole new medical challenge. I had slipped several discs in my lower back, and those discs were pinching my sciatic nerve. In other words, what I had was not so much a back problem as it was a nerve problem—and it was debilitating. Instantly, my life became a hamster wheel of painkillers, medical specialists, and physical therapy, but nothing worked. From the moment I woke up, my back pain was so severe that I couldn't even put my shoes and socks on, because I couldn't bend over. If I was in any position other than vertical, pain would shoot through my body. I had to lean against the wall just to get my underwear on. Once I was vertical and highly medicated, I could function, but my walk was more like a shuffle. On a typical day, I would swallow eight or ten painkillers just to get through the day. Between the Vicodin and the Dilaudid and the morphine, I was as high as a kite all day long. Moreover, in yet another twist on the "sick man's diet," I lost sixty pounds. Because of the pain medications, I had no appetite; I couldn't eat, and I was withering away. I had constant stomachaches, as well as the shakes. My eyes were black, my skin was ghostly white. And I was still in pain. Finally, after spending almost a year in this drug-filled nightmare, I realized that there was no other option: it was time for back surgery.

The procedure itself was uneventful, and I was sent home the same day. Unfortunately, I was sent home without the anti-nausea medication I needed to be taking to counteract the side effects of the painkillers. Christina and I had agreed that I would spend my recovery time in our first-floor bedroom. Meanwhile, she was pregnant again, and her pregnancy had become complicated, so she was at the emergency room worrying about a miscarriage. It turned out to be a night that neither of us will ever forget. Very fortunately, Christina got the care and attention she needed. Back at home, I began throwing up. Because of the pain medication, and the lack of nausea medication, the room was spinning. The physical act of vomiting was beyond excruciating, because just hours before, I had been under the knife, and I had fresh wounds. So, to stop throwing up, I stopped taking the pain medication—which created a new kind of constant pain. Then it got worse. The catheter they had inserted at the hospital caused my urethra to close up. It should have been checked before I was sent home, but it wasn't. My urethra had swollen shut. I would shuffle to the toilet, but then I would just stand there, leaning against the wall in agony: I couldn't produce anything. No matter what I did, I couldn't get relief. I couldn't go to the bathroom. This went on all night, from bed to toilet to bed and back to the toilet, with no relief.

By 6:30 in the morning, I hadn't slept all night, and I was screaming. It was obvious that my bladder was about to explode, which was something I hadn't considered during the night. Realizing I could actually die, I grabbed my phone and called 911. The ambulance took me back to the hospital, where the ER staff discovered that the swelling of my urethra had caused a complete blockage. Once that was solved, they wanted to send me home, but I told them that something about my back still felt wrong, because I had been in so much pain the night before. They kept trying to get rid of me, but I refused to leave. When you know something isn't right, you have to fight for yourself and go with your gut. They insisted, and I kept refusing, until finally I was readmitted upstairs to the actual hospital. It turned out that there were, in fact, some unexpected complications from my back surgery. Those problems were eventually put right, but not before I had spent another week in the hospital. Then it was back home, for a second attempt at recovery.

———

Recovering meant lying flat on my back in our downstairs bedroom for weeks. I felt useless. The dark self-talk came at me again, filling me with despair. I would lie there watching sports, basically channel-surfing from one thing to another, but nothing made me feel any better. By the time I'd been in that bedroom for six weeks, I was lonely and depressed. Meanwhile, Christina was fully occupied and in charge of all the responsibilities of running the household.

Stuck in bed, drugged up on painkillers, and looking for a distraction, one day I found myself watching a marathon of the TV series *Intervention*.

It's a show about the efforts that families of addicts go through to get their family members help. In the show, some people make it, and some people don't. I watched an episode, and that episode became another one, and then another one, and I couldn't stop watching. For hours I lay there watching. I found myself feeling more and more inspired. *They did it*, I thought. *I can, too.*

I told myself, *It's time to move.* I had been in that dark and lonely room for six weeks, and I hadn't moved. I hit "Pause" on the TV remote. Then I told myself, *You're going to walk to the front door.* So I slowly rolled out of bed and put one foot on the floor.

Then the other foot. I slid both feet into my slippers. And I stood up.

Next, I shuffled to the door of the bedroom. So far, so good.

I kept going. I made it to the front door, a distance of about sixty feet.

Once I was at the front door, I thought, *You've made it this far. Why not keep going? Let's see if you can make it to the corner.*

I hadn't planned on going beyond my front door, so I was still in my pajamas and slippers, and I had left my cellphone in the bedroom. But I pulled open the front door and took a step. Then another one. Bent over and shuffling down the street, I'm sure I must have looked like Mr. Burns from *The Simpsons*. But I ended up walking all the way to the corner of our street.

Then, something special happened. I started to feel less pain; I felt looser. After a few more steps, I was no longer hunched over; I was standing up straight. Once I got to the corner, it occurred to me that this was the first time I had moved in six weeks. I said to myself, *You know what? Screw this. Just keep walking.* And that's exactly what I did. I did a complete loop of the neighborhood, a total of two miles, in my pajamas and slippers. When I walked back into the house, Christina was freaking out. I hadn't told her that I planned to go outside, let alone take a two-mile tour of the neighborhood, so she had been calling everyone in my family, asking them, "Have you heard from Tarek? *Has anyone heard from him?*" But she could see that I was doing better: a whole lot better. In fact, when I finished my walk, 90 percent of my pain was gone, which I'm convinced was the result of all that movement. And that was the very first step of my recovery. I once again had hope that through hard work, I would be able to get my life back.

If I had ever doubted it before, I knew it then. You've got to start moving and keep moving. Take one step. Then take another one. Basic stuff. It all creates forward movement.

CHAPTER ELEVEN

TAKE MASSIVE ACTION

By the end of 2015, Christina and I had a lot to celebrate. That fall, Christina gave birth to our son, Brayden James El Moussa, and I was reminded of another basic truth: there is nothing better in the world than seeing your own child smile at you for the first time. Meanwhile, we had completed four seasons of *Flip or Flop*—almost sixty individual episodes—and the show was attracting millions of viewers. Many Thursdays, we were number one on TV. The show was surpassing even our wildest dreams. We marked the milestone by buying a fifty-one-foot yacht that we proudly christened the *Flip or Flop*.

Physically and mentally, however, I was nearing rock bottom again. In hindsight, I'm certain that my body was still reacting to the loss of my thyroid gland and to my new reliance on synthetic hormones. Anyone who has been through thyroid cancer can tell you that it always takes the doctors some trial and error to get the mix and the dosage right. Until that happens, it's not uncommon for patients to go through some combination of anxiety, depression, sleep disruption, brain fog, and fatigue. I experienced every single one of those side effects, but I didn't yet understand the connection. At the time, all I knew was that my cancer treatments were behind me, and I had recovered from the back surgeries, but I was utterly exhausted all the time. It felt as if someone had draped me in a stack of those lead blankets they put on you for an X-ray. Every morning, with hours of filming and work scheduled for the day, I struggled just to get out of bed. And the exhaustion was constant. I was hauling my body, and those imaginary lead blankets, through the day, desperate to get home. I would lock myself in my home office, staring at the walls. It felt like I was trying to get through the day on one hour of sleep—not six, not three, but one—all the time. It was a very vicious cycle that I lived every day, and it took a tremendous toll on my mental health.

Southern California has more than its fair share of Doctor Feelgoods. It seems that in every strip mall there's someone with more greed than compassion: they slap a fancy diploma on the wall, they promise you miracles, and they eagerly take your money. I didn't know any of this the first time I walked through one of those doors. I thought I was about to get help from a legitimate doctor. When my exhaustion got to the point that I was worried about even being able to work at all, I was desperate to listen to—and pay—anyone who might give me my energy back.

After talking with Christina, I agreed it might be a good idea to go see a bioidentical hormone doctor. On a day that I will regret for the rest of my life, I stopped in at an "anti-aging" clinic: the kind of place whose stock-in-trade is Botox injections and dermal fillers. The doctor listened to my concerns, and I told her about my history with cancer. Then she explained that my exhaustion was obviously a consequence of my testicular cancer. All I needed was a boost in my testosterone. And she had just the thing. At that point, a tech came in. He looked like he could bench-press 500 pounds; he was definitely on testosterone. He brought out a huge needle, marked a little "x" on my butt with a Sharpie, and showed me how to inject myself with synthetic testosterone. On top of the testosterone injections, she instructed me to inject myself daily with vitamin B12 mixed with a fat burner; human chorionic gonadotropin, or HCG, which was supposed to increase testosterone production; and an estrogen-blocking pill. When she also recommended human growth hormone, or HGH, I declined, because I knew that people with a history of cancer should not take that. This "consultation" lasted thirty minutes at the most.

Just to be clear, this was an MD, giving me the product as a prescription. But the MD was practicing way outside her field of expertise. She assured me that this miracle product, the testosterone itself, was "nothing like steroids." Of course, that's exactly what it was: an anabolic steroid. The next thing I knew, I was stabbing myself, daily, with what I believed was nothing more than a testosterone pick-me-up.

Almost overnight, I started feeling like Superman: stronger, faster, unstoppable. Every morning, I was leaping out of bed, excited to go inject myself. I would hit the gym for two hours and be thrilled with the obvious changes in my body. I was immediately addicted to this drug and the way it made me feel. But the truly sinister aspects of the drug were there, too, on full display. Steroid survivors will tell you that your whole mentality changes. At times you become extraordinarily egotistical, cocky, and a full-blown narcissist. At other times it's as if you're a zombie, barely aware of your surroundings.

And that's exactly what I experienced. I felt like the king of the world, but also lonely and depressed, at the same time. My "highs" were off the charts: a level beyond euphoria. But the lows were terrifying, and my mind was playing tricks on me. I would be seized by anger and despair at random moments, and for no reason. I started having panic attacks. Sometimes, my heart started skipping beats, and I thought for sure I was going to have a heart attack. I was so concerned, I started wearing a heart monitor. At times, my heart would be pounding away at 130 to 140 beats per minute, revving way too high. The only real solution would have been to quit the testosterone—which I didn't understand at the time. Frankly, I don't even remember that period very well. A lot of my memories of it are murky and confused, as if it happened to someone else.

What I do remember, vividly, is thinking that I was losing my mind. I felt so alone, so depressed and angry, that I couldn't function. I would come home and be so strung out, so raw, that I couldn't even talk to Christina; I couldn't talk to Taylor or play with Brayden. I would walk upstairs and close the door. I would sit in front of my computer, thinking about nothing. More often than not, I'd sit there simply staring at the wall. I was a terrible husband, father, friend, and son.

———

Daytimes were still about the work. The flipping business was going strong, and the staff could run it without my full-time attention. And by this time, I had other successful ventures up and running. I was making more money than I ever thought possible, which had always been my dream, and at the same time, I was the most miserable I had ever been in my life, because of my struggling mental health. Christina and I knew that we were committed to this amazing ride for as long as the ride would last. But between the show, the businesses, the filming, our babies—and my self-administered "treatments"—the ride had gotten wilder and faster than we could really handle as a couple. The bigger our media stage became—and by now, it was huge—the less energy, focus, and attention we had to spend on each other. We would see our pictures on magazine covers and entertainment websites, and we'd want to believe that we really were that joyful-looking couple in the pictures. But we knew better. Things between us were tense, but I never thought for a moment that we would separate.

One afternoon, after an especially heated confrontation with Christina, I went out to our backyard in Yorba Linda and hopped over the fence. I craved some exercise. Behind the house is Chino Hills State Park, a huge wilderness area. I had just ordered a couple of mountain bikes, and before the bikes arrived, I wanted to scout the trails close to the house. I texted my neighbor to see if I could borrow his bike, but he wasn't home, so I decided I would have to hike it. Chino Hills is known not just as a place of rugged beauty, but also as a habitat for mountain lions, bobcats, coyotes, and rattlesnakes, and I was heading out late in the afternoon, meaning I might be out there after dark. A few weeks prior, I had received my California concealed-carry license, which involved taking classes and getting a background check from the sheriff's department. So tucked inside my backpack, along with multiple bottles of water, was a .38-caliber "insurance policy": my pistol. In my wallet was my concealed-carry license.

For the first thirty minutes, my hike was going great, and I found awesome trails. The day was hot, and I soon worked up a sweat, so everything was going as planned. I stopped to take my shirt off. Then I heard the loudest *chop-chop-chop*, and I looked up and saw a helicopter. My first thought was that something was wrong, and there might be a fire; after all, this was a fire-prone area. Then a police officer leaning out of the helicopter pointed a rifle at me. Dust swirled around me from the spin of the blades, and a loudspeaker crackled, "Get your hands in the air!"

Suddenly, off-road police vehicles roared up, and a dozen officers leaped out with their guns drawn. They began screaming, "Get down! Get down!" And all I could think was, *What the hell is going on?*

About two seconds into this ordeal, I heard an officer shout, "Tarek?"

With my hands still in the air, I screamed back, "Yes! I'm the guy from TV! What are you guys doing?"

They immediately lowered their weapons and told me to get to the ground.

As it turned out, the helicopter was responding to a 911 call from Christina. After our blowup, she had seen me stuff the pistol in my backpack as I stormed out our back door. Now the chopper, and several other police units, were searching for a "possibly suicidal male." Other than that, the officers didn't know who they were looking for.

Just seconds after all of this began, the officers determined that no, I was not suicidal. But, following protocol, they put me in handcuffs, and they escorted me home. For the next several hours, I sat on a cooler on my driveway, handcuffed, while the police tried to figure out what was going on. At the officers' request, I voluntarily surrendered all my guns, which I got back later. No charges were filed, and the police vehicles drove away. And that was the very last time we were together as a family: with Christina walking down the driveway, crying, and me sitting there in handcuffs, asking myself, *What in the world is going on?*

Looking back, I can see why Christina was so concerned. In the weeks leading up to that terrible day, my mental health was as bad as it had ever been. But ending my life was just something I wouldn't have done.

Christina asked me for space for a few days, and she wanted me to leave our home. Thinking I would be back soon, I grabbed a few personal items, and off to our boat I went.

Deep down, I knew the testosterone was to blame for most of my issues, but I was addicted to the stuff. Yet this whole ordeal was enough for me to take drastic action. Within hours of leaving the house, I was already taking massive action to fix the problem. The very next day, I quit the testosterone, on my own, cold turkey.

———

"A few days" turned into two weeks alone on the boat, and I went downhill fast. Soon I was curled up in my berth for long stretches of time. I wasn't eating or drinking, and I was paralyzed with despair. As I learned later, quitting testosterone cold turkey creates havoc with your hormones. The biochemical shock made my emotional upset much, much worse. Without really understanding what was happening, I was experiencing the biggest emotional trauma of my life, and I needed professional help.

I've talked in this book about the importance of having a "crew" in your life, about how vital it is to have a group of collaborators and supporters to rely on. And at this pivotal moment—when I wouldn't have cared if that boat had broken free of its moorings and carried me out to sea—my crew stepped in to make sure I was okay. One day, six or seven of my friends stopped by the boat to spend some time with me. I hadn't eaten, I was obviously depressed, and I was drinking heavily. Out of nowhere, I passed out. When I came to, I was lying on the deck, and my friends were staring down at me. One of them said, "We need to get you some help."

One friend happened to be personal friends with Dr. Drew Pinsky, who specializes in the treatment of addictions and mental health issues. He's known as Dr. Drew, and by then he had already been hosting his own TV show for several years. My friend called Dr. Drew and explained to him what was going on with me. When it was my turn to talk to Dr. Drew, all I really remember saying was, "I need help."

Dr. Drew made it clear that I needed medical and emotional support. He offered me an immediate referral to a round-the-clock, seven-days-a-week inpatient facility. I eagerly accepted. It would be a chance for me to show my wife I was willing to do anything to get my family back.

I checked myself into the facility, which was a halfway house occupied mostly by heroin addicts. Suddenly, I was under twenty-four-hour care. I was subject to a curfew. I had to make my own bed. I had to do my own laundry. For the first time since high school, my life was governed by someone else's rules. The only time I was alone was when I went to the bathroom, and even then, someone stood by the door.

This extremely structured environment turned out to be exactly what I needed. I lived at the rehab center for two months, and during that time—away from the glare of the spotlights—I talked to several therapists. Every day consisted of regular support sessions and counseling. It would be hard to put into words how grateful I am for the many, many kindnesses—and frankly, the tough love—that I experienced there, from that first phone call to Dr. Drew to the many counseling sessions at the center. When I left, I still had a ton of work to do. But those two months gave me enough to keep fighting for my life.

REEVALUATING

I leased a home for myself and my kids in Newport Beach. I was back in the city where I had first bottomed out. This time, it wasn't my apartment that collapsed, it was my life. Just as they had for years, the paparazzi waited outside the house, more eager than ever to capture an embarrassing photo or moment. Every time I opened the door, I was blinded by camera flashes and bombarded with questions. I spent so much time inside that house it started to feel like quarantine all over again.

Now that Christina and I were sharing custody of our kids, Taylor and Brayden were with me on a regular basis, and it would be hard to put into words how much I looked forward to being with them. My years of going all out on my career, plus some serious medical and emotional chaos, meant that I had never really been that close with my kids. Now, all of that changed for me, in a very powerful way.

Since Brayden was only eight months old at the time, a nanny helped me take care of him. Taylor was five and already full of personality. Spending time with her and watching her laugh and play became the highlight of my week.

Still, there were days when I didn't want to get out of bed. Sometimes I thought about quitting the TV show, just shutting everything down and giving up. But then I would see Taylor's smile or hear her laugh, and I would tell myself, *This is what matters. You can't quit. Look at who you're doing it for.* Whenever Taylor noticed I was sad—which was often—she would smile and say something like, "It's okay, Daddy, everything's gonna be okay." And I would think, *Man, I've got these amazing kids. I've got to keep going.* Whenever I spent time with them, I felt a little lighter, a little stronger. I began to be more motivated. I realized how precious and important my kids were.

Today I know that one of the main reasons I made it through this awful period of my life was my kids, and Taylor in particular. Taylor and I had never been that close before this, but now, suddenly, you couldn't separate us. It was one of the most powerful flips I've ever experienced. And she became my best friend.

———

You hear about people staying inside their "comfort zone," but sometimes I think it should be called a *discomfort* zone. Passive acceptance of a bad situation can start to feel comfortable. Stuck in a bad relationship, or a crappy job, or any number of other bad situations, people begin to "adapt" and accept. They become comfortable being uncomfortable, and that's no way to live. It's like living in a smelly house for so long that you no longer notice the smell. The negative situation is a constant strain in your life, but you're used to it. It has become so familiar that you think of it as normal.

That's why, from time to time, you need to check in with yourself and ask: Am I living in a "comfortable discomfort zone"? Have I allowed myself to grow accustomed to circumstances that don't make me happy, and never will?

Living like a hermit in that rented house, I allowed my emotions to control me for a while. Feeling like a failure started to feel normal. I quit noticing that I had slipped into self-talk straight out of the fixed mindset "script": *You don't deserve this. It's totally unfair that you got cancer. It's totally unfair that your marriage blew up. Life is so unfair.*

The worst thing about this kind of thinking is that it gives you no tools for bouncing back. There's no way forward. Fixed mindset thinking says, if you flunked the first test, you might as well drop out; you're a failure. Give up. In my case, for months, the "solution" was just to stay indoors all day. I had successfully completed my inpatient care, and my health was better, but I was a long way from being recovered. Had it not been for those regular visits with my kids (thank you, Taylor!), I would have given up.

Thankfully, I found myself going back to a basic rule, a "flipping fundamental": *Distressed means opportunity.* Just as overgrown grass and piles of garbage are often promising signs to a house flipper, emotional distress can be the starting point of a personal flip. It took me a while, but eventually I turned my emotional turmoil into the motivation I needed to start getting my life back. My anger and hurt prompted me to take the small steps—one after another—that led to my recovery. Eventually, those small steps turned into huge leaps and bounds. But if I had never taken those small steps—the kinds of steps that so many people hesitate to take—I never would have reached those leaps and bounds.

Back to basics. *If you can't undo the situation, what can you change? Where else in your life can you exercise control? What small steps can you take, right now, that will get you headed in the right direction?*

It was all about relearning things I already knew. I remembered that first visit to the gym with Justin—a small step that ultimately transformed my life. I remembered jumping in the car—taking action—to close my first big real estate deal. Put simply, what I relearned was this: when you find yourself living in a "discomfort zone," it is far, far easier to take action—to do something physical—than to spend another minute trying to "figure things out." You can sit on the couch trying to fix your own head, obsessing about your problems, or you can get your ass off the couch and do something about it. Whatever the problem is, you've got to get going, because the longer you wait, the worse it is.

The beauty of taking action is that it gives you progress. It demands your time and attention. It forces you to think about what you're *doing*, not how you're feeling. So if you discover you're living in a "discomfort zone," find out why that is, and go take action. Find something to focus your time and attention on: specifically, *something to do*. Making that small adjustment forces you to pay attention.

The first step, for me, was picking up the phone and calling doctors, one after the other. I knew I had to come to grips with my medical situation. If I was really going to flip my life, I absolutely had to start feeling better; I had to get my energy back. And I was going to do whatever it took. So I made it my job to search for the right doctors—legitimate ones, professionals who could figure out what was really wrong. Before all of those testosterone injections turned me into a monster, they had seemed like a quick fix to my underlying problem, my constant exhaustion. Now I got busy trying to find out, the right way, why I had felt so exhausted in the first place. I set out to fix the problem, not just put a Band-Aid on the problem.

This work of reaching out to new doctors paid off in a spectacular way. Just as I had hoped, they discovered what the real issue was, and it had nothing to do with my testosterone. In fact, these doctors assured me that there was nothing wrong with my testosterone level: at 580, it was exactly where it needed to be, naturally, even after my operation for testicular cancer. They told me I never should have been on testosterone in the first place! My real problem was hypothyroidism. Even though I had been faithfully taking T3 thyroid medication for years, I was undermedicated and I had no thyroid. So the doctors immediately increased the amount of T3 medication I was taking—they almost doubled the dose. Then they added a prescription for T4 medication, which turned out to be a game-changer.

Almost immediately—after years of testosterone hell—I felt like a new person. This combination of T3 and T4 made me feel as if I had come back from the dead. Within weeks, I went from feeling groggy and lifeless to wanting to get up and get active. I was still sad and depressed, but physically, at least, I could feel myself getting my life back.

My next step was one that helped me get outside my own head. Every day, without fail, no matter how depressed I felt, I drove myself to a hot yoga studio. I forced myself into that hot yoga studio for a one-hour session every day. A miracle would happen in that room. I would be so hot and exhausted during the class that my personal struggles were the last thing on my mind. I was just trying to survive the hour without throwing up. When the class ended, the sense of relief I felt lasted for a few hours, making every second in that room worth it.

RENOVATING

On a late summer afternoon in 2016, as I came home from work and pulled up to the house, I realized I just wasn't ready to be home alone. So I stayed in my car and kept driving. I had no destination; I just drove around the neighborhood in circles.

I found myself at a red light on Balboa Boulevard in Newport Beach. Surrounded by a picture-perfect landscape, and by happy people on the boardwalk, I was miserable. I was screaming out loud about all the things that weren't fair in my life: getting cancer, the separation from Christina, not seeing my kids whenever I wanted, all of it. For months, my mind had been spinning with one thought: I don't deserve this. It's unfair.

Then, suddenly—still sitting at that intersection, I heard myself saying, *Life isn't fair. Bad things happen to good people every day, and there's nothing they can do about it.*

And that right there was the turning point in my life. I told myself, *Stop bitching and complaining. You can't do anything about the past, but you sure as shit can do something about the future.*

In that moment, I felt my anger subside, and relief started to take its place. A sense of calm came over me. For the first time in a very long time, I had hope for the future. Once I acknowledged that life wasn't fair, it gave me the power to immediately start focusing on building my new life. I knew it would take time to get over my terrible sadness, but I was no longer a prisoner. There was no point in obsessing about the past, allowing deep sadness to be my prison. It was time to get free.

Sitting at that light, I made the conscious decision to start thinking about the future rather than living in the past. At last, I could see a way forward, a chance at a new life. A new idea took hold: that I could rebuild and reinvent myself into someone genuinely better, stronger, and more alive than I'd ever been. I knew this would be the biggest challenge of my life, but I also knew I could get there. Through hard work and massive action, anything is possible.

And the light turned green.

CHAPTER TWELVE

DOUBLING DOWN

One immediate commitment I made to myself was to start having fun again. For ten years, I had been so busy and so stressed, working and grinding and coming home and going to sleep, over and over again, that I had forgotten what it felt like to have fun. Now, finally, I had the physical energy and the desire to start enjoying life.

For almost an entire year after my separation from Christina, I kept myself isolated from the people I had known in the past. Instead, I began seeking out new friends and hanging out with a new crowd. My old friends meant well and reached out to me, but for a while I couldn't bear the memories that surfaced whenever I was with them. It was just too painful. I ended up interacting with almost no one other than my family members, Roger Behle, and Pete de Best. Reconnecting with the rest of my "crew" would take longer. They were confused about why I stayed away. The truth is it just hurt too much to be around anything that reminded me of my old life.

Meanwhile, I remembered the things I had loved doing as a teenager, and I started doing them again. I started racing go-karts. I made it up to the mountains to go snowboarding. Every few days, my new friends and I would load up and head out for a few hours of fun. And yes, I even bought a dirt bike. I was roaring through the desert again thinking about nothing except the next dune.

I found myself taking Taylor and Brayden to Chuck E. Cheese, a lot—sometimes, three days in a row! That atmosphere, where the three of us could simply laugh and enjoy each other—felt comfortable and safe. I couldn't help noticing how dramatically things had changed from just a few years earlier, when all I could do was stare at the walls—when I would try to play with Brayden, or talk to Taylor, and I just couldn't do it. Now, as if by magic, I realized that I was actually present for them, engaged and listening and thrilled to be in their company. That became a conscious goal for me, one that I framed as an affirmative, positive statement of what I wanted: *I want to be here, in every way, for my kids.* And I've never stopped.

———

Christina and I were still under contract and filming the show, but of course the atmosphere on the set was awkward, to say the least. The production team did their best to keep things positive, efficient, and professional, but for months on end, the energy was terrible. Every time I was on the set, I told myself, in so many words, "You're gonna get through this." It was about sticking with the basics and taking it one small step at a time.

Day by day, I began to look ahead again. My internal conversation became: "Keep moving forward. Time heals everything."

Gradually—taking stock of how good I felt during those drives up and down Balboa Boulevard—I made a point of going places, seeing people, and "checking in" with old friends and making new ones, and I even made some attempts at dating. I quit hiding from the paparazzi. I started going into the office on a regular basis. After each visit, I noticed how much better I felt. As time went on, I started dreaming and setting new goals again. As 2018 drew to a close, I started coming up with more ideas for businesses.

———

I had made it through two different cancers, an awful back surgery that stole over a year of my life, a testosterone nightmare that literally ruined me, and the collapse of my marriage. After all this, I finally arrived at a point where I was okay. Things weren't back to normal, by any means, but I no longer felt like I was in a destructive spiral. And for a while, it felt good to be safe.

But gradually, as the weeks turned into months, I decided that "safe" was no longer a destination. For one thing, I foresaw that someday *Flip or Flop* would end. That ride would be over, and I would still have major bills to pay. Just as importantly, by making a game out of starting businesses, I would be taking action. I could stop wallowing in sadness and think about something new. Now that I had climbed out of a dark hole, I was finally ready to "jump upward," to seize opportunities to expand the scale and scope of what I was already doing. I made the decision to get to the next level. I knew it would be a ton of work, but it would distract me from the past.

Like a lot of businesses, real estate consists of different specialties and different roles. Fundamentally, property gets transferred from one party to another—it's sold or leased or gets passed some other way, such as by a will. However, beyond that very basic definition, the business involves so many variations—and so many ways to make money!—that when someone says, "I'm in real estate," it really doesn't tell you much. You can sell houses, you can buy houses, you can develop houses, you can build high rises—the sky's the limit. You can make one dollar, or you can make a billion dollars. It all depends on how big your goals are.

At the lowest level, being a real estate agent, you're trading time for money. You're on a "commission treadmill," in the sense that you're always chasing that next commission check. If you want to go to the next level, it becomes a little more difficult: once you become an investor and start flipping houses, you have to raise money, you have to get loans, and you have to manage contractors. But there's more opportunity there, too; you can make more money. From there, you might decide to do real estate syndicating, meaning you're pooling money together from investors to buy projects anywhere from $1 million to $1 billion, and maybe even more. At this level, you're playing in the "big leagues" of real estate.

My own career in real estate is a case in point: starting out as a buyer's agent, I showed buyers condos in the city of Rialto, California, that were listed for $50,000. Rialto is a long drive from where I lived in Orange County. It would take me over an hour to get there, and then I would drive people around all day, showing them those condos. I spent so much on gas that by the time I got my commission check, I was losing money! To top it off, many times, after I had shown my clients dozens of places—which took me hundreds of hours—they would call me to say they had bought something with someone else! Then I learned that I could do a lot better for myself by becoming a listing agent. I did that by looking around at my "comps," the highest-performing agents at my office. I didn't know how to become a listing agent, and that's when I attended my first Mike Ferry event and decided to focus on expired listings. That was followed by a stint of doing short sales during the Great Recession of 2008, before I jumped to the investment side as a house flipper in 2010.

There's nothing wrong with any of these different specialties or approaches, and I'm not here to criticize any of them, because I've done all of them, and I've learned from them! But I can't help noticing how often people in business—and in life—choose the safe choice. They stay with what feels familiar, versus betting on themselves and trying to accomplish more. There's pain in change, and the more pain you can endure, the further you can go. The more often you experience pain and fight through it, the more comfortable you become with it. You rewire how you think about pain! Eventually, what was uncomfortable becomes comfortable. But you have to make a start.

What if, by taking a couple of steps in a different direction, and being a little uncomfortable for a while, you could reach more success in all aspects of your life—more success than you ever thought possible? Believe me, I know a lot about negative circumstances. Sometimes, external circumstances make it difficult to change. More often, though, the refusal to make changes is about something else.

I'll apply this concept to the flipping business. It often surprises people to learn that there are really two different kinds of flippers. A wholesale flipper is really just "flipping paper." They find a motivated seller, someone who's ready to sell; they agree to a price and get a contract signed that has an assignment clause, giving the buyer the right to assign the contract to another party; then they immediately assign that contract to a fix-and-flip investor who buys the house. The wholesaler makes the difference between what the seller agrees to sell for and the third-party buyer agrees to buy for. For example, suppose a seller agrees to sell me a house for $300,000, and I find a buyer who will pay $330,000. As the wholesaler in this case, I get to keep the $30,000 difference between the two contracts, and the buyer that I find is the one who buys the house from the seller. In other words, wholesalers never buy the house, which minimizes their risk—but they also leave a lot of money on the table that they could have made by rehabbing and selling the home themselves. Their goal is to make quick money. And it's one of the best ways to get started in real estate if you have no money. This is one of the first things I teach at Homeschooled by Tarek.

The other kind of flipper is the one who actually buys, fixes, and sells the house. They buy the property, they renovate it, and then they sell it to a homeowner or a buy-and-hold investor. For this flipper, the process takes longer—sometimes, much longer—than a wholesale flip. But, of course, the ultimate goal is the same: profit. And most times, you can make a lot more money fixing, renovating, and selling than you can wholesaling. Many times, the opportunity is much larger, but so is the risk. That's because you actually own the real estate and you have skin in the game. If something goes wrong, you can lose real money.

Now, again, people in the business have different objectives, and there's nothing wrong with the wholesale side. I wholesale properties, too, if that's what the market indicates I should do. But I often wonder why more wholesalers don't move on to the next level. When you've established a successful career as a wholesaler, and you've built up some resources—money, connections, and know-how—maybe it's time to move over to the "owning" side. Why not make that shift, knowing you stand to make much bigger profits?

The answer, I believe, is fear. Most people are scared to take the next step. But in life, you can't be scared to take the next step! You have to keep taking those steps, one after the other. That's the only way to grow. It all boils down to that fundamental difference between a fixed mindset and a growth mindset. If you have no option right now other than being a wholesale flipper, that's one thing. On the other hand, if you've stacked up enough experience and resources to go bigger—if the only thing keeping you from becoming a fix-and-flip investor is your own self-concept, your limiting beliefs and fears—then that's a different story. At that point, it's no longer a business problem; it's a mindset problem.

Whether you're flipping houses or flipping your life, you need to figure out what changes will get you to the next level. Look around for that one thing you need to get there, one thing that will move the needle in the right direction and help you go much bigger, much further than where you are now. If it's about becoming a house flipper, join a mentorship group (like Homeschooled by Tarek!) that can teach you how to do it. If it's about getting healthy, start working out; start taking vitamins and eating right. It may be uncomfortable for a while, but the discomfort doesn't last. Over time, the pain goes away, and the pain turns into... excitement! The excitement comes once you start seeing results. You begin to want more and more of those results.

Once you find those positive things, double down. Turn those behaviors into habits. The foundation of all success is creating routines, positive things that you can do on a daily basis. A lot of them will be painful at first, but *you give them everything you've got*, and you never quit until you reach your goals.

—————

That's where I was as 2018 turned into 2019. I turned my attention to scaling up my businesses. Tarek Buys Houses, the flipping business that Pete de Best and I had started together in 2010, was going strong. With Pete and Adam Lindholm handling day-to-day operations at TBH, the company had survived the storm of my personal struggles, but not without a fight. At this time, I decided to double down on TBH and grow the business, which took a ton of energy and focus. All that work started paying off, and the business was growing. Then there was Next Level Property Investments, the holding company that Pete and I had formed years earlier for the rental properties we were buying all over the country. It, too, was flourishing: Next Level was buying dozens of rental properties per year, and we were now managing about two hundred houses.

I was determined to go beyond this level and launch new brands and businesses. With each new idea, I started to look around for "comps": something or someone to emulate. Just as I did when I first jumped into expired listings at age twenty, I started to be curious about which of my different ideas would work. Once I found that out, I committed myself to doubling down and giving it everything I had. The results were three new brands. But before I found success with these new ventures, something totally unexpected and wonderful happened. To my complete surprise, I found myself falling in love.

EVERYBODY JUMP!

Woody's is an iconic bar in Newport Beach. Thanks to its history and its location overlooking the harbor, it's "the place to be" on the Fourth of July, but it's almost impossible to get a boat slip there for that celebration. Somehow, on July 4, 2019, I got one. As I pulled my boat in, the sun was shining and the party in front of Woody's was in full swing. Music was blaring, and young women in bikinis were entertaining the crowd by tossing fire sticks back and forth.

On my boat were a handful of friends. I had told myself that this was a day simply to "recharge" and enjoy some downtime. Meanwhile, I certainly wasn't thinking about starting any kind of serious relationship. I assumed it would be a long, long time before I met someone special, if I ever did.

I had docked the boat and was in deep conversation with one of my guests when a group came over from the boat next to mine. Out of the corner of my eye, I saw a gorgeous young lady in the group. Seeing her there, slim and blonde and beautiful, I stopped talking, mid-conversation. Instantly, I found myself imagining what life could be like with her. I made a beeline toward her, held out my hand, and said, "Hi! I'm Tarek." She smiled and said, "Yes, I know who you are. I'm Heather." I silently congratulated myself for the amazing fringe benefits of having a TV show—until she said, "You asked me out two years ago. Don't you remember?"

Trying desperately to maintain my "cool guy" persona, I asked her, "Where?"

She responded, "Instagram."

I asked her to hold on for a second. Turning my back for a moment, I raced through my Instagram account and discovered that, sure enough, I had reached out to Heather Rae Young two years before, but she had explained then that she already had a boyfriend. I immediately spun back around and asked her, "Hey, still got that boyfriend?"

"No," she said.

"Okay, good," I said. "Want to go to Paris?"

"Absolutely not," she said.

"How about Las Vegas? Separate rooms?"

"No," she said. "I know how that works."

Running out of options, I said, "Fine. How about dinner?"

And she smiled and seemed to be thinking long and hard about it. Then all she said—still smiling—was, "Maybe."

Soon our conversation moved to serious subjects. Within minutes, both of us were aware of the chemistry between us. Heather had grown up in a loving family in humble surroundings, a no-stoplight, one-post-office mountain town east of Los Angeles. Like me, she was accustomed to working hard; she had been doing so since she was fourteen. Like me, too, she had started out knowing nothing about real estate, and then, in her twenties, she had earned her license. She had thrown herself into the job, and over the next three months she sold not one, but two multimillion-dollar homes.

Talking about the similarities in our backgrounds, our careers, and our struggles with recent relationships, it was as if we'd been friends for a long time. And even though the boat was now jammed with partygoers, it felt as if Heather and I were alone. But not for long. An intoxicated twenty-something heard one of us say the word "divorce," and she charged over to us and blurted out, cheerfully and at the top of her lungs, "There'll be no more of that talk! There'll be no talk of divorce!"

Immediately, the intimate connection between Heather and me was destroyed. When I looked around, Heather was already leaving my boat and was on her way back to the other one. She was deeply bothered by the drunken interruption, and so was I.

I retreated downstairs, feeling melancholy. I felt as if I had lost a major opportunity. Heather and I had had the beginnings of a wonderful conversation, and I wasn't ready for it to end, not by a long shot.

I realized I couldn't stay downstairs alone feeling sorry for myself. When life shows you an opportunity, you've got to go for it. It was time for me to jump.

I ran back upstairs to the party. Looking out the windows, I could see Heather laughing and talking with some good-looking guy on the front of the boat next to mine. I knew I had to do something to get her attention, but I didn't know what it was. Then it hit me. I dashed into the wheelhouse of my boat and found the button labeled "Horn." I pushed that thing like I had never pushed it before: a long, loud blast. Heather, her male admirer—and everyone else, on all of the boats!—jumped and stared.

I stuck my head out the window, and with a big smile, I yelled to the guy, "That's *my* girl!" Then I walked out onto the deck. "I just claimed her!"

Heather laughed, and so did the guy. One blast of a boat horn—and my yelling like a crazy man—was all the hint he needed. Still laughing, he excused himself, and soon Heather and I picked up where we had left off. I got her phone number, and before long, we were communicating regularly. A couple of weeks later, we had our first date. A few days after that, we moved in together. We were married in October 2021.

With any business, the road to success is full of bumps, but I never imagined what it would take to get one of my first ideas from 2018 up and running. Homemade Investor was inspired by the coaching experience I had at age twenty. I knew how much coaching had helped me, and in 2019, I decided it was my turn to pay it forward. As with any good comp, the rule of "emulating" says, Do what your comp does, but see if you can do it better: emulate and *enhance*. Aim even higher. I thought about all the things I didn't know when I started investing in real estate, and I wanted Homemade Investor to be a way for me to communicate those things better and faster for new investors.

Once I had figured out the content of the training, I signed a deal with a company that was eager to host Homemade Investor events, not just in the United States, but all over the world. These events would be in big, impressive venues that could hold thousands of people. We agreed to a five-year deal that promised to generate substantial fees, and I couldn't wait to start sharing what I knew with would-be investors. The very first event was to happen in Honolulu, Hawaii, in March 2020, just weeks after the Homemade Investor brand was officially launched. So in March, Heather and I went to Honolulu, and while we were there, we noticed that the TV news started to be about one thing, and one thing only. For the first time in our lives, we heard the term "COVID-19." All around us, people were starting to wear masks.

My first reaction—like a lot of people's—was *What the hell is going on?* When Heather and I got home, things got worse. The company that was hosting my Homemade Investor events—the one that had committed to a five-year, multimillion-dollar deal—alerted me that they were strictly in the business of hosting live events, and suddenly, they couldn't throw live events. Thanks to the pandemic, my amazing deal with them had collapsed overnight.

Whenever you find your route blocked, move sideways. Don't be like the kid who starts climbing that jungle gym, finds the path blocked, and then quits. Instead, look for the pivot or adjustment that will open up your path to the next level. Keep telling yourself, *When you never quit, you never fail. As long as you keep trying, you're still on the road to success.* Never stop looking for a way to keep climbing.

I had to pivot, immediately. My "pivot" was to quit worrying about when, if ever, live events might happen again. Instead, I saw that—using the power of the internet—I could launch my program online, and I created Homeschooled by Tarek, an online real estate course that would allow real estate investors to learn from me and some of the most successful coaches in the industry—people as inspiring and informative as Mike Ferry and other experts had been for me. I also knew that for this training to be meaningful, I needed to be heavily involved; I needed to be the head coach.

Today, I'm proud to say, we have a highly regarded program, one that squeezes decades of real estate expertise into six months. Every week, for two hours at a time, I'm on a live webinar with my students, sharing with them my twenty years of industry experience and knowledge. Homeschooled by Tarek empowers them to take action and find deals. Without question, there were bumps in the road launching Homeschooled, and it almost didn't happen. What began as a "pivot," going online in response to the global health crisis, has become one of the program's greatest strengths.

———

Another seed that I planted back in 2018 is The Agentcy by Tarek El Moussa at eXp Realty. My goal for The Agentcy was to build the largest real estate organization in the country, a network of thousands of agents who benefit from the best marketing strategies and training in the industry. Today, I'm hitting those goals, and we have more than 1,400 agents in the organization. Let's just say that The Agentcy is an upgrade—a massive one—from the Wise Ol' Owl training tapes that I watched day after day decades ago.

———

A third business idea grew out of comments I'd been hearing ever since *Flip or Flop* had started airing. For years, people who knew about the show had been reaching out to me to say, "Tarek, we want to invest with you. We want to buy deals with you." I didn't need to take anyone else's money just to flip a house; the projects weren't big enough, so I had always turned them down. But I had never forgotten those offers, and now that I was ready to "double down" and go even bigger, I started thinking about how to partner with other investors. The idea I had was to launch a private equity real estate firm that acquired commercial real estate.

When I told my "inner circle" about my idea, all of them said I was crazy.

"You're a 'house guy,'" they said. "No one's gonna do commercial deals with you. You're wasting your time. It's not going to work."

You may remember that I had heard exactly these kinds of comments way back in 2003, when I had first gotten into real estate. I'd heard them again in 2010, when I first started flipping, and then again when I wanted to do a TV show. "It won't work! You're crazy!"

And just as in 2010, I firmly believed that my idea *would* work, for three reasons. First, I was convinced that the Tarek El Moussa "brand," which up to that point was all about houses, was transferable. I felt certain that the brand now had enough credibility, goodwill, and enthusiasm behind it to carry over into the commercial world. Second, those offers from would-be investors hadn't stopped. On the contrary, more people than ever were telling me, "Hey, let me invest with you!" I couldn't justify partnering with other investors just to flip a house, but I sure could if the target property was a three-hundred-unit, $50 million apartment complex.

Third, the more I thought about the idea, the more "comps" I saw. Wherever I looked, I saw heavy hitters in commercial real estate, people who had figured out how to create ownership entities, raise money on a huge scale, and then buy multimillion-dollar buildings for themselves and the investors who partnered with them. To put it simply, *I saw that they were doing it, so I knew it could be done.*

So I jumped. I was smart enough to know that there were things I didn't know, and I recognized how much I had to learn. Private equity isn't just about real estate; I had to build an entire company. So I got busy learning everything I could: about syndicating, about private equity, about all the things it takes to make these commercial deals happen. You might say that instead of watching VCR tapes at the Wise Ol' Owl, I was taking massive action on my own program of "self-study." At the heart of this self-study was figuring out how my comps—other syndicators in this field—had done it. Just as you do with any comp, I made it my goal to understand how, exactly, they accomplished what they did. I needed to do everything I could to translate their achievements into operational steps, actions that I could take myself. For that to happen, I knew I would have to reach out to them, and I knew I would have to be persistent.

I started by searching the hashtag "multifamily" on social media. I studied posts from different people all over the country. One by one, I looked through their posts and read their bios. Whenever one of them looked like a promising comp, I would reach out: "Hey, my name is Tarek El Moussa. I love what you're doing. Can we connect?" Sometimes, it was a phone call: "Hey, this is Tarek El Moussa. I'm excited to see what you've been doing, and I'd love to talk to you about it." It was all about leveraging my name recognition to open doors and get conversations going.

Once we connected, I didn't hold back. Straight up, I asked for help. I asked my new contacts about everything I needed to know: "So how long have you been doing what you're doing?" "Was your business hard to set up?" "What's the most important thing somebody starting out should know?" This was no longer about sitting at the feet of somebody like Gary Lucas, passively admiring my comp, but ending the conversation with no idea what to do next. With every conversation, my goal was to identify another action step, another goal for me to pursue.

The result, ultimately, was TEM Capital, my commercial real estate company. We partner with accredited investors to purchase commercial opportunities nationwide. In essence, we form LLCs that buy multifamily, self-storage, and other commercial properties all over the country by pooling investors' money together. Just as with Homeschooled—and any other business!—there have been "bumps" along the way. Success doesn't happen overnight. But today, I'm proud to say that we are partnering on multiple $50 million projects. That's quite an upgrade, I think, for someone who twenty years ago was living in an apartment with no walls. And, of course, I can't help thinking how far things have come since those six miserable weeks in 2007, when my boss in commercial real estate insisted on calling me "Derek."

———

If my life has taught me anything, it's that you've got to plant seeds, and the only way to plant seeds is to get started. You never know which seeds will grow, so plant more than one, give them some water, put in the work, and then wait for those seeds to sprout! I know I'll keep coming up with ideas—that's what an entrepreneur does. And as stressful as it is at times, I love turning my crazy ideas into something special.

Now it's your turn to jump. It's your turn to set goals and start chasing your dreams. If a broke kid from Buena Park can build a global brand, you know that dreams can come true. That means it's your turn to shock the world! Take a step, then another one, and never stop. Keep putting one foot in front of the other.

EPILOGUE

Closing the Sale

Throughout this book, I've said I was a work in progress. It's still true. The flip that I'm proudest of, by far, is me, the person who's talking to you in these pages, but I know my personal flip isn't finished. I'm reminded of one of my dad's trademark expressions. Sometimes, as a kid, after I had mastered a particular skill in baseball, I'd be ready to quit for the day; I figured it was time to celebrate. But if there was still daylight—if the sun had not yet set on the baseball field—my dad would give me a little pat on the shoulder and say, "You're just getting started, kid." And we'd work a little longer. I've come a long way, but I'm still jumping, I'm still grinding, and I'm still trying to figure things out.

Long before we finished filming *Flip or Flop*, I got serious about looking for the next opportunity. When I found out that Christina was filming a show called *Christina on the Coast*, I knew it was my time to develop a show of my own. In the spirit of "doubling down," I came up with the idea for a whole new flipping show, one that would help novice renovators get in the game. We called it *Flipping 101 with Tarek El Moussa*. Instead of Christina and me flipping houses, *Flipping 101* put me in the role of coach, teaching rookie flippers how to do flips. Once again, there were doubters. People with authority let me know that they didn't think much of my idea. So it felt as if I was starting over. I knew some things about TV, of course, but with this new concept, I was going solo. I had to put everything on the line and prove myself all over again. When the pilot aired and the ratings came back, I was thrilled. My new show was a hit. This is a success I'm especially proud of, because at first there were those who didn't give the show great odds. But I also know I gave it 10,000 percent of my energy and effort—and it worked. All I needed was the opportunity.

My cancers have been in remission for about ten years now, and, thankfully, my doctors tell me that at this point, the chances of them coming back are slim to none. Meanwhile, I have regular checkups, including extensive testing, just to be sure. It took a while for my physical energy to come back to where it used to be, but I'm happy to say that the sensation of walking around under those "lead blankets" is a thing of the past. I'm enjoying a level of physical well-being that I thought I might never have again. As I write this book, my health is the best it's ever been. I have truly flipped my life.

That makes it a particular thrill to hear people ask me, "Tarek, where do you get your energy from?" The answer is the same as it has always been: from having lots to do and getting excited about reaching my goals. When I *don't* have a thousand things going on—when I don't have lots to do—that's when you'll see me start to fade. In that respect, not much has changed: when I get bored, I run out of energy; I go flat. Knowing that about myself, I plan to continue doubling down on lots of different fronts. I'll never stop looking for new ways to go bigger and better.

I also know that, sometimes, *the only way to get something to go right is to learn what makes it go wrong.* I expect the occasional disappointment or setback, but I try to stay on the lookout for "the good inside the bad." Even today, I have my share of ups and downs. Who doesn't? The difference is, if I'm feeling down, I tell myself, *You'll get through this and feel fine. You have experienced way worse.* And I know I will. Deep down I know the feeling will pass, and I can get through anything.

I try to remember that the challenges life throws at you are difficult enough, without you trying to deal with them all by yourself. If my experiences with cancer, and financial shocks, and out-of-whack hormones, and headlines of divorce taught me anything, it's that there are always people who want to help. I'm very fortunate to have a "crew" around me who help me think, act, and feel in ways that are human and appropriate to the situation. They help me maintain that balance between tenderness and cooperation with my family and friends, on the one hand, and the strength and determination I need to compete and win in the business world, on the other. It has taken work. It takes a lot of hard work to find the right people and bring them into your life. From reading my story, you know that you have to be willing to go through a lot of bad ones in order to find the good ones. But you can't give up.

From time to time, all of us need someone to tell us to put our shoes on and get to work. All of us need someone who not only celebrates our victories with us but helps us figure out how to double down on them: how to enhance and capitalize on those victories. For more than three years after my marriage fell apart, I was essentially alone in that respect. I did what I could to be my own cheerleader. Then, Heather came into my life, and miraculously, I found myself saying things like "we" and "ours," instead of "I" and "mine." Heather became my constructive cheerleader, just as I try to be hers. In their hit song "One Man Band"—the song Heather and I chose for our wedding—the music group Old Dominion captures it for us. The song talks about two people becoming one, with one partner laying down the beat while the other carries the tune. When

Matthew Ramsey sings, "I don't wanna be a one-man band / I don't wanna be a rolling stone alone," Heather and I know exactly what he means. We are now united as a couple, both onscreen and off. As I write these words, we have just wrapped the first season of our new show, *The Flipping El Moussas*, and we hope the fans are loving it. Best of all, I'm beyond excited to be "doubling down" now that Heather and I have expanded our family even further, with the addition of Tristan Jay El Moussa, who arrived on January 31, 2023, making me an official father of three!

Today, my ARV—my personal vision of success—is very much about building an incredible future for my kids. Thankfully, there's a night-and-day difference between the father I was when Taylor and Brayden came into the world and the father I am today. I'm determined to be the best father I can possibly be, for all three of my kids.

Meanwhile, my daughter, Taylor, reminds me of myself—a lot. She can't sit still, she goes full speed ahead, and she doesn't hesitate to tell you what she thinks. I have to be careful walking through doors at our house, because Taylor is likely to be hiding on the other side, ready to smack me in the face with a pillow.

Not long ago, Brayden was learning how to ride a two-wheel bike. Remember how scary that was? Brayden and I had been working on it together for a while, and one day, I released him, and he pulled away. He was pedaling away down the street, and it was amazing—and then he fell over. Bike and Brayden lay there in a big heap. As I ran toward him, thinking he might be hurt, Brayden pulled himself out of the wreckage. He had this look of fury on his face; then he said, very passionately, "Practice, Dad! *More practice!*" Which I believe was his way of saying, "Quit? Hell! I'm just getting started!" I couldn't have been prouder.

Three sets of grandparents are active and present in my kids' lives. My parents drop by on a regular basis, and it's a thrill to watch my kids learn soccer from my dad—one of the all-time greatest coaches and a passionate lover of the game. Brayden is starting to "get it"; meanwhile, Taylor is a better soccer player than I ever was. In a way, we've come full circle: Dad picks Taylor up, takes her to the soccer field, and coaches her. Soccer has become their shared passion, something both of them truly enjoy.

Mom is now "cuckoo" about her grandkids—so much so that she has acquired the nickname "Coucou." And, speaking of bicycles, recently we bought Taylor a bike—just the right color, exactly what she had asked for: the perfect bike. Taylor loved it. And so did my mom. If fact, my mom admired Taylor's bike so much that she went out and bought an identical one for herself! And suddenly, Taylor didn't love her bike so much. After seeing her grandmother riding up and down the street on the same bike, Taylor decided her bike wasn't cool anymore. I don't think any "parenting handbook" has a solution for that one.

Don't tell Angelique, but I'm also very proud of my big sister. An entrepreneur herself, Angel owns her own very successful salons—two of them—right down the street from my office building. Always motivated, always hardworking, she embodies the spirit of relentless renovation. Her beautiful daughter, Malia, is Taylor's best friend.

These days, I'm going all out on new business ideas, including the ones I described in the previous chapter. Among other goals, my "ninety-day sprints" include some pretty intense learning goals, and I'm working with multiple people to help me assemble just the right teams for the plans I have in motion. Check back with me in a couple of years to see how these new projects have worked out!

———

I haven't said much about "meaning" or "purpose" in this book, and that's by design. When you set out to flip your life, it can be very hard to know what will provide you with meaning—to know what your "purpose" is. At nineteen or twenty, I couldn't have told you what my purpose was.

Instead, I've tried to emphasize how important it is to identify a life that excites you, to look, *hard*, at someone else who's living that life, and then to throw yourself into activity that brings you closer into alignment with that "comp," that model for what you want to do. Sometimes, putting all of that together can be difficult. But I'm convinced that it's much easier and more productive to take those actions than to try to figure out what your purpose is. In fact, I'm convinced that you have to take action first in order to discover what your purpose is! The day will come when you arrive at a sense of meaning and purpose; you'll eventually get there. Meanwhile, don't waste time and emotional energy obsessing over your "destiny," or waiting for some flash of insight. Take action.

Let me share with you one more fundamental rule of flipping. It goes like this: *A successful flipper is willing to spend their own money fixing up the neighbor's house or yard if it looks bad.* When you improve a house, you improve the neighborhood. So you go next door; you offer to have the neighbor's yard mowed, or you get their trash picked up, or you get their house painted. It doesn't have to cost much. But the result is that a buyer's perception of the whole neighborhood goes up. In the process, your own flip house becomes more valuable and attractive, so everybody wins.

I've learned that when I do what I can to help someone else, both of us win. I'm not talking about sacrificing my own ARV, my personal life goals, in favor of someone else's. I'm saying that whenever I can help another person move toward their own ARV, their big dream, there's something deeply satisfying about that activity. By adding value to both their ARV and mine, I get to enjoy something extremely gratifying—and, yes, meaningful!

I'm a product of some really good coaching—from the time I started playing baseball and soccer as a kid all the way to today—as you know from reading my story. In many cases, I'm the one who took a gamble and put myself into that coaching. And nothing is more satisfying to me than participating in someone else's success, encouraging them, bringing someone else along. I love helping people tap into something they didn't know they had. It's as good as watching a kid hit that first home run or score their first goal. Whether it's my own kids or my colleagues in real estate, my favorite thing to do in the world is to motivate people: to lift them up and convince them to believe in themselves.

There is genuine satisfaction in helping others clean up their messes or "jump higher" in life. Nothing is more exciting than seeing other people achieve their dreams, because it allows me to relive those moments with them! The trick is to inspire them to actually *do it*—not just think about it, but actually do it. It's what one of my own comps, Mike Ferry, did for me. I'm determined to do it for others. And today, that's where I get my meaning and purpose.

In real estate, this part is called the "close," and my "close," to you, is simply this. Treat your life as an investment property. Treat it as a house with tremendous potential. Make the decision to transform that property into something spectacular—a life that is full of happiness and success—by taking massive action on the steps I've laid out for you here. Yes, you're going to encounter unexpected challenges, and at times you will want to quit. But don't. There is light at the end of the tunnel. You just have to make it there. Commit yourself to remodeling and remaking yourself, over and over again as the years go on, renovating relentlessly.

And now you know. For years, I couldn't get any traction on my big dream, the ARV that I had for myself twenty years ago. Ironically, the big dream I had then—the one I thought I would never attain, and then did!—is so much more modest than the dreams I have today. It turns out that there are levels to this game, and right now—like you!—I'm on the hunt to get to the next level. And like I always say, I'm just getting started.

THE END

APPENDIX

Use the following quizzes and exercises to help you evaluate your own "flip project"—meaning your life as it is right now!—and start to implement the kinds of renovations I talk about in this book.

By the way, this work is private. A long time ago, I learned to do my house flips from the inside out. I focus on the interior repairs before I turn to the outside. I know the best way to get the highest price for a house is to wait to show it until it's remodeled and staged—when it has reached its highest potential. Before that moment, people don't really understand what they're seeing, so any comments or opinions they might have are irrelevant and unhelpful.

The same goes for these self-assessments and exercises: your answers are for your eyes only.

SELF-TEST FOR CHAPTER ONE: DOUBLE-CHECKING YOUR LOCATION

Put a check next to each statement that describes you:

_____ Nobody gives me a harder time than I do; the person who is the most critical of me is me.

_____ I worry that my "best years" are already behind me.

_____ I can't remember ever being so absorbed in doing something interesting that I lost track of time.

_____ I don't feel I'm making progress toward any particular goal.

_____ If my life turned to shit tomorrow, I can't think of a single friend who would be there for me: a person who would take me in, come get me, take me to the hospital—whatever.

_____ If there's one word to describe my life right now, it's "boring."

_____ Every day, I find myself desperately looking around for something new and different.

_____ My romantic life sucks or is nonexistent.

_____ This week, I've spent more time looking at social media than talking with my actual mouth.

_____ Fear is a big issue for me; I have more fear than most people do.

_____ More than once, I've been involved in a toxic relationship: a person in my life has been abusive or manipulative toward me.

_____ More than once, I have found myself in situations that became, or were about to become, violent.

If you checked seven or more statements, then you and my nineteen-year-old self have a lot in common. Take heart! As I say throughout the book, all good flippers know that "distress means opportunity"—and I am living proof of how dramatically better things can become. The Tarek I introduced to you in Chapter One would have checked most of these boxes. But a whole lot has changed for me in the years since then—just as it can for you.

SELF-TEST FOR CHAPTER THREE: ASSESSING YOUR FOUNDATION

Try this quick test. Which of these statements do you AGREE with?

1. _____ If I take care of myself, I can avoid illness.

2. _____ Whenever I get sick it is because of something I've done or not done.

3. _____ Good health is largely a matter of good fortune.

4. _____ No matter what I do, if I am going to get sick, I will get sick.

5. _____ Most people do not realize the extent to which their illnesses are controlled by accidental happenings.

6. _____ I can only do what my doctor tells me to do.

7. _____ There are so many strange diseases around that you can never know how or when you might pick one up.

8. _____ When I feel ill, I know it is because I have not been getting the proper exercise or eating right.

9. _____ People who never get sick are just plain lucky.

10. _____ People's ill health results from their own carelessness.

11. _____ I am directly responsible for my health.

These statements come from a test—the Multidimensional Health Locus of Control (MHLC) Scale—that is used in the medical field to study the relationships between patients' beliefs and their health. It may seem strange that I've asked you to do what sounds like a "medical questionnaire," and make no mistake: I'm not offering medical advice here. But the fact is that your results here say a lot about *how much control you believe you have over your own outcomes.* If you AGREED with 3, 4, 5, 6, 7, or 9, there's work to be done in the area of your self-concept. As Chapter Three makes clear, taking ownership of your own outcomes is the foundation on which you build success.

EXERCISES FOR CHAPTER FOUR: FINDING YOUR "COMP"

Because I believe that emulating a comp—the focus of Chapter Four—is so important, I've come up with this three-part exercise that I hope will help you do just that. It's the sort of self-assessment that I wish I had done twenty years ago. The three parts need to be done in order. The first two parts focus on you: they are designed to help you dig deep and get to know yourself better. Then and only then should you go on to the third part, which I hope will help you identify your own "comp" and then take action!

Part 1: Understand

For each of the following items, circle the number between 1 and 5 on the scale that most closely describes where you put yourself.

1. Assume it's a typical Thursday afternoon. Looking ahead to Friday night,

1	2	3	4	5
I have the evening planned out: I know pretty clearly where I'll be, with whom, and when.		I have some vague plans, and I expect the specific details to come together in the next couple of hours.		Figuring out Friday night is for Friday night!

2. Staying with the scenario in the first question, whom do you expect to actually make the plans?

1	2	3	4	5
I generally rely on someone else, such as a friend or partner, to put a plan together; typically, I go along with whatever they decide.		It's collaborative: a group text or other group discussion is usually how we decide what to do.		Typically, I'm the one making the plans for the group; my idea for how to spend the evening is usually the one that others go along with.

3. Same scenario: it's a typical Thursday afternoon. Which is most likely to describe you?

1	2	3	4	5
I'm looking forward to "staying in" tomorrow night, after a crazy week at work; some much-needed quiet will allow me to unwind and relax.		I look forward to having dinner with a friend; others may join us, but at the most it will be four of us, enjoying good conversation over a great meal.		After a crazy week at work, I feel like I'm ready to burst; I can't wait to head out the door and blow off some steam!

4. Friends want you to come out with them all day Saturday to do one of the following activities. To which of these possible choices are you most likely to respond with "Awesome! Can't wait!"?

1	2	3	4	5
Wine-tasting tour of some local vineyards.		Guided float trip down a local river, noted for its beautiful scenery and some occasional rapids.		Bungee jumping off a bridge over that same local river.

5. Suppose I'm about to ask you to describe five moments in your life when you felt like a failure. More specifically, I'll ask you to describe where you were; who you were with; what happened to cause you to feel that you had failed; and finally, who said what. How long would it take you to come up with those five "Fail" episodes with that level of detail?

1	2	3	4	5
As I sit here right now, I can barely remember one! I'll need a lot of time for this.		I'm sure I can remember five episodes. Just give me about ten minutes to describe them.		I'm ready to tell you all about all five of them, in detail, right now.

6. You are self-employed. At a party, you're introduced to a mid-level manager at a local company. She mentions how difficult it has been to fill a vacancy in her department. The two of you hit it off, and she ends up asking you to come in later in the week to interview for the job, which involves working directly for her. The job pays 10 percent more than what you're currently making. You:

1	2	3	4	5
Enthusiastically accept the manager's invitation, knowing you can decide later whether or not to accept a possible offer.		Ask for some time to look at your schedule, knowing you'll use that time to find out all you can about the company and the manager.		Politely decline, confident that you're just happier working for yourself.

7. There's a particular song you like to sing in the shower, and you know all the words. Tonight, you've stopped by the local pizza place to pick up your order. There's a decent-sized crowd tonight. Just as you're cashing out and getting ready to leave, "your" song comes up on the karaoke machine. You:

1	2	3	4	5
Wink at the cashier, stroll over to the machine, pick up the microphone, and let it rip.		Scan the crowd to see if any friends are there to give you "moral support" as you step onstage.		Grab your takeout bag, do a little dance, and get the hell out of there.

Comments: Don't be surprised if most of your responses to these scenarios are 2s, 3s, and 4s, since it's rare for people to land on one of the extremes—either 1 or 5—for every question. You might also be saying, Well, sometimes I'm closer to 1, and other times I'm closer to 5. Your goal here should be to recognize which end of the spectrum most accurately describes you personally *most of the time.*

Question 1 has to do with how much planning, organization, or regulation you need before you feel comfortable starting an activity. Applied to the working world, some careers attract people who are careful planners—for example, engineers, military people, doctors, and lawyers who get a lot of personal satisfaction from their jobs are more likely to choose 1 here. These are people who really don't want to start a project without first having a plan for how they're going to get it done.

At the other end of the spectrum—those more likely to choose 5 for this scenario—are the more spontaneous, creative, even impulsive people—artists, teachers, entertainers—who seize on an idea (or two, or three) and then pursue those ideas, happily and productively, in a loose, free way—a way that their more "organized" friends would describe as chaos. Speaking for myself, I know I'm at the far right end of this spectrum. People around me will tell you that I have a million ideas, all the time. I'm thinking constantly about new opportunities, new projects; then, as soon as an idea starts to crystallize in my mind—no matter what time of day or night the idea hits—*I stop everything and start doing it.* I've learned to rely on a trusted "crew" of highly organized people (1s, on this spectrum!) to help me keep all of it structured and under control.

The point is that you want to know where you land on this spectrum. Before you start a project, are you someone who needs everything to be "just so," or do you prefer to just *go*?

Questions 2, 3, and 4 all point to how much sensory stimulation you feel you need. People whose answers fall between 1 and 3 in these situations are more likely to perceive the messages or sensations they get from the outside world as being already plenty loud: their personal "default setting" causes them to experience the world as "noisy" and full of sensation. As a result, they crave peace and quiet. By default, they've already got all the sensory input they can stand. They don't want any more.

People who answer 4 or 5 on these questions perceive the world just the opposite way: as flat, dull, boring, and unstimulating. As a result, they crave excitement! They need stimulation, and they will do what they can to get it. These are the people who can't wait to get to the club. They're hungry for the loud music and the flashing lights and the swarm of moving bodies. They tend to drink more and smoke more and gamble more than other people; they're more likely to drop everything and run off to Vegas in search of stimulation. They engage in high-sensation, often high-risk behaviors—motorcycling, skydiving, rock climbing—as a way to "turn up the volume" of life, since their default setting feels to them like it's too low.

Smoking, drinking, motorcycle riding—and yes, running off to Vegas on a whim!—have all been part of my résumé. There's no doubt in my mind that I'm someone who needs to crank up the volume of life in order to compensate for that sensation of things often feeling dull or flat. But not all the time! Many times, I can't wait to kick back and enjoy some quiet privacy, away from the crowds. So, yes, I lean toward option 5 on these three questions, but not every moment of every day.

Question 5 touches on a tendency that all human beings have: our "negativity bias," our tendency to interpret too many things in our lives as bad, and not enough of them as good. Evolution has hardwired us to stay alert to threats, which is important for survival; however, this tendency can also cause us to react to bad things faster, more strongly, and longer than we should. Answering 3, 4, or 5 on this question suggests that you may be holding on to negative thoughts in a way that interferes with your ability to move forward. Your negative thinking may have become automatic. And—as I point out in Chapter Three—those thoughts are probably inaccurate! If you answered 3, 4, or 5 here, make your next goal a *physical action*—the kinds of activities I talk about at the end of that chapter—that will give you that "small win" you need to break free of this negative momentum. When you start moving, you're moving in a positive direction.

Question 6 challenges you to get honest about how well you do in situations where someone else is setting the rules. I was fortunate to learn, early in my life, that the traditional working world can be a painful environment for people like me. High-energy, hyperactive "sensation seekers" have a hard time taking orders from a boss; we're action-oriented, bottom-line, gotta-run types, and we tend to be miserable when we're not in charge. So while most people would probably give an answer between 1 and 3 on this one, put me down for a 5.

Question 7 is somewhere between a 3 and a 5 for me—maybe 4½. If that's surprising, consider this. When I'm on camera, filming a TV show, I have zero anxiety. My focus is on the actual flip project and all the things we need to accomplish; the camera just happens to be there. I'm moving around, and the camera is there to capture me in action, doing what I do, so I don't even think about it. I also know that I didn't achieve this comfort level overnight; I worked hard at overcoming my fears. I've gotten a whole lot better at it than when we filmed the first episode of *Flip or Flop*, but it took work. Finally, I know that being on camera is my job; it's what I do to make a living. Giving in to anxiety is not an option.

So for me, the "karaoke" scenario in this question isn't going to deliver the emotional payoff that someone else might get from it. Hearing my song, I'm more likely to nod my head with the beat a couple of times, grab my food, and get out of there. As for option 3, I might get up and sing if my friends dared me to, but even then they'd have to pay me...which (knowing my friends) they probably wouldn't!

When you've finished this little quiz, I hope that you and I can agree on some things. First, there are no "right" answers. Your answers are your answers. Each item represents a range of possible answers, from one end of the spectrum to another. A second important takeaway is that *this quiz is about your features, not your limits*. It's about understanding some things about yourself—your preferences, your style of approach—that can, in turn, guide your thinking about what you may need to change in your life in order to have more happiness and success.

Part 2: Engage

Here's an exercise that goes directly to another one of those all-important building blocks that make you who you are. Grab something to write with, and don't move on until you have written, honestly and completely, your answer to this assignment. Once again, what you write is for your eyes only. No one else needs to see what you write.

Here's the question: *When was the last time you were so absorbed in what you were doing that you completely lost track of time? Exactly what were you doing?*

This activity needs to be something you found to be both *difficult* and *enjoyable*: it challenged your abilities in a way that you found gratifying. In simple terms, this activity was hard for you, but in a good way.

Being unaware of time passing is an important clue that what you were doing was a rewarding activity for you and that you were fully engaged in doing it. It may have felt as if you were in a "zone": you were so focused on the work to be done that you weren't really thinking about how to do it, or what you were feeling—instead, you were just *doing it*.

Speaking for myself, I know that hustling T-shirts, and trying to figure out how to make money brewing beer, and yes, even twirling my medieval skirt for tips, all provided me with moments of "being in the zone." It wasn't true all the time, but there were definitely occasions when—with any one of those activities—I was so involved in it, so engrossed in doing something difficult but enjoyable—that I lost track of time. Those kinds of experiences are important for you to have and important for you to keep track of.

Part 3: Who Is Your Comp?

Now we come to the nitty-gritty. Your goal in this exercise is to identify a "comp" of your own: someone in your life, or someone in the world, who can turbocharge your confidence about the direction you should be going in. This person embodies that "ARV," that after-repaired value or personal vision of what success looks like for you. Finding your comp requires you to take account of the things you've learned about yourself as a result of doing Parts 1 and 2 above.

By the way, this exercise is, again, just the kind of assignment that I wish someone had given me twenty years ago. And, once again, the work you do here is for your eyes only.

Step #1

Think about a person you admire.

This person can be living or from the past. The person may be known to you personally, or could be someone you know a lot about in some other way—from social media, the internet, books, whatever—but it must be a flesh-and-blood human being, not a fictional character or avatar or something like that.

Now answer the following question: *What does this person have that I want?*

This is about describing the life that person enjoys, using your own words, and paying particular attention to what about that person's life strikes a chord inside you.

Here's a "pro tip": Write a detailed answer to the question. Give yourself a goal of at least three sentences here. That's because you want to gather as much detail as you can. There's no need to overthink this, but you do want to be thorough. If you can't come up with at least three sentences, something's wrong! You need to put more work into finding a comp for yourself!

If you've read Chapter Four, then you can probably guess what my younger self would have written. I would have picked Gary Lucas, and my answer might have sounded like this:

Gary owns an apartment complex and more than twenty-five houses. He's wealthy. Now that the complex is fully renovated and occupied, Gary and his wife are going to be doing great financially. They're going to be set. Gary has the know-how and the "game" to continue growing his wealth. He's on his way to doing it over and over again.

Step #2

Now answer the following question: *What's so interesting to me about that person's interests?*

Write at least three sentences here as well. Notice that, to answer this question completely, you'll need to understand both (1) what interests the person you're writing about, and (2) *how those interests line up with interests of your own.* Let this question trigger some serious thinking about the similarities between you and your comp.

My own answer might have been something along these lines:

Gary is a gambler. That sounds like me. He's passionate about the "game" of real estate investing. He loves the thrill of taking risks, knowing how much is at stake. He makes it sound intense and exciting. Like me, he's interested in the numbers: how much to invest, how to measure the return on his investment. All of that is interesting to me, too.

Step #3

Next question: *What abilities does my "comp" use on a regular basis that I have, too?*

Your goal here, again, is to write as much as you can, making sure that you "dig deep" to find parallels between you and your comp. As best you can, you want to identify the personal resources that your subject taps into on a regular basis.

Caution: Beware of getting sidetracked by thinking that this question is about "talent." Even if you don't have what people call "talent," you can make a million bucks a year—if you're willing to work your ass off! Through dedication, determination, and hard work, people can go way farther than they think—with or without talent.

For now, just see whether you can figure out what kinds of personal tools your subject uses every day and how those line up with yours.

As an example, my answer might have been:

Math. Gary makes quick calculations all the time. Whenever he's talking about one of his deals, I've noticed that "the numbers" are always an important part of the story. I do that, too.

Another "tool" I see in Gary is his love of competition. He's all about the contest between himself and other investors, between his businesses and the competition. I get that. That's how I see things, too. I can imagine myself saying, "You think you're going to buy that house before I do? Watch this."

Another tool: seeing two or three moves ahead. When Gary comes out ahead in a deal, it's often because of that ability to anticipate what the other person is going to do. I love that kind of strategic thinking; I think that way, too.

Step #4

Write your response to the following: *What is this person doing, or what have they done, that I can do right now?*

Don't be surprised if this is the most difficult question for you. It certainly would have been for me. That's because, unlike a dream, this question is framed in terms of an actual event or behavior. You're trying to isolate an actual activity that you can do. This question leaves you no "out": it forces you to think about your comp in terms of operational steps, meaning how they got to where they are. It's about *doing*, rather than talking about doing. It forces you to define your own "flip" in terms of an operational step, a procedure.

Here's an example of what I'm talking about. From time to time, people I've met who are just starting out in real estate will say to me, "Well, you know, Tarek, you have this amazing Rolodex. You know all these people; you have all these great contacts. To make a deal happen, you can just pick up the phone."

And my response is, "Yeah, that took work. Building up that Rolodex of contacts took me about ten years of nonstop grinding."

In other words, those people overlook my operational steps. They mistakenly believe that it all just happened somehow. They're confusing the "dream" with the effort it took. My operational steps included getting referrals from one client to another, asking every contact for the name of another potential contact, and so on. I had to put one foot in front of the other, over and over again.

Dig deeper. Think about the house flipper who's comparing the project house to the comp house down the street. That flipper is thinking about that comp in terms of the checklist of steps that the other owner went through before listing the renovated house for sale. It's about the series of individual steps or incremental improvements that brought that comp house to the condition that it's in now. Now apply that thinking to your own comp. This question is about homing in on that next step, *the very next action you can take*, that aligns with what your comp has already done.

Step #5

Aim high enough for it to hurt.

As a result of carefully studying your comp, you should now have a personal goal for yourself. You know what to do, and you believe you have what it takes to accomplish it. You feel confident that you have both the knowledge and the ability to complete that task. Now comes another "self-check" you need to perform.

Make sure you frame your activity goal, your action step, to be both as *specific* as you can make it and as *difficult* as you can make it.

Here's what I mean by "specific." Instead of just saying, "I'm going to do my best," you want to tell yourself, "I'm going to go all out on this activity, for X number of days (or weeks, or months). By the end of that time, I'll know whether it works or not." Give yourself a specific deadline for discovering whether or not this activity "clicks" for you in a positive way.

That's how I have approached my goals throughout my career, and it's how I do it today. My "ninety-day sprint" in 2003, when I turned myself into an "expired-listings machine," is an example. And I'm convinced it's how you should do it, too. Choose an activity, and give yourself a deadline for knowing whether or not it works.

And make sure that what you're about to do is a serious test of your ability. You want to set things up in such a way that you know it's going to get uncomfortable for you—not impossible, but genuinely difficult. Ask yourself, *Is what I'm about to do as hard as it can be for me?*

Give yourself a goal that is difficult enough to be meaningful. You'll know you're heading in the right direction when you find yourself thinking, *This sounds hard. What happens if I succeed?* Let it be so challenging that you're curious about whether you can pull it off! Remember that, ultimately, you want to both emulate *and enhance*: you're chasing after that "comp," that person you admire, with the goal of someday surpassing them! There's no question that, as a kid, I looked at Gary Lucas as a dazzling model of success. Then, after doing everything I could to emulate Gary, I looked around and discovered there were levels to the real estate game far beyond what either Gary or I had imagined, and—to my amazement—I had positioned myself to experience those levels.

Step #6
Jump! Just jump!

I've thought a lot about why people freeze when it comes to going after their goals. Often it's the result of setting a big goal, but then neglecting to set smaller, more incremental goals that can move them toward that bigger goal. So please don't leave Step #5 until you know what you're going to do, and for how long, in order to find out whether it works or not. Then throw yourself into that incremental sub-goal.

For example, say you want to become a house flipper, and the goal is to flip your first house. In order to arrive at this big goal of flipping a house, you need to accomplish smaller sub-goals along the way. The first goal is: find the house! A sub-goal of that sub-goal might be taking classes to learn how to find a house. Then you need to get the money to buy that house. Maybe that means you've got to go find an investor. That becomes your next sub-goal. And so on.

If your big goal is, "Get physically fit," find the next small step you can take that moves you in that direction. Maybe the first sub-goal is cleaning up your diet. Another sub-goal might be spending thirty minutes at the gym this afternoon.

Approach this the way a flipper does: first, I'm going to do this; then I'm going to do that; after that, I'm going to do this other thing. Stack your sub-goals to achieve your main goal. Treat each sub-goal as being just as important as your main goal. After all, if you can't find the first house to flip, you'll never become a house flipper. If you can't clean up your diet, you'll never get healthy and fit. Give yourself smaller steps along the way to that ultimate ARV, your personal after-repaired value. Then give each of those sub-goals everything you've got!

By the way: Don't wait to make sure you've chosen the "perfect" goal. If you do that, you'll never get started. If a goal excites you, it's good enough. If the activity strikes a chord in you, in the ways we've already talked about, it's good enough. If someone who's a lot like you—your comp—has already done this kind of thing, then you know it can be done; it's good enough. Finally, you may need to tell yourself that there is no "perfect" choice anyway. So don't wait for that perfect choice. Quit worrying about it. Pick an activity, and then go for it! Jump!

And that brings me to what may be the most important thing I've discovered about goal setting. Once you have a goal, you need to start on it! Immediately! Find out whether it works!

If that sounds obvious, consider how many times you or people you know have made grand plans, or have "formulated ideas," or built castles in the air, and then done nothing. I know people who never go from *I want to* to *I'm going to*. They stay stuck at *I want to* for years! Whereas I'm at *I want to* for about five seconds. Then I move to *I'm going to* right away. In almost the same instant that I say *I want to*, I'm going! I throw myself at my next goal immediately. I give it everything I've got.

ACKNOWLEDGMENTS

The biggest thank-you to my wife Heather and my kids, Taylor, Brayden, and Tristan. Tay and Bray, you got me through the toughest period of my life, and I couldn't have made it without you! You gave me the will to keep going as my life was falling apart. And Heather, you changed me from the inside out. You taught me to believe in love again, and you inspire me to be better every day!

Heartfelt thanks to my parents, Bill and Dominique. Dad and Mom, you came to this country in hopes of creating a better life for yourselves and your future family. I want to tell you that you accomplished that goal. Everything I have today came from the lessons I learned watching you throughout the years, and I couldn't be more grateful. You taught me what it means to be a good human and a hard worker, and you gave me all the support I needed to accomplish my wild and crazy dreams of success. You mean everything to me.

Thanks to the "crew" who helped me turn my dream of a book into a reality. Jonathan Leach and my amazing book agents, Todd Shuster and Jon Michael Darga, were there from the beginning. I also thank my outstanding team at Hachette: Dan Ambrosio, Sean Moreau, Sheryl Kober,

Kathy Streckfus, Annie Lenth Chatham, Erica Lawrence, Nzinga Temu, Lauren Rosenthal, and Kara Brammer brought their expertise and passion to this project, and I'm grateful.

Finally, a big thank-you to Roger Behle, Pete de Best, Adam Lindholm, Brad Pearson, Annette Flores, Brittany Roker, all the incredible people from my various companies who work with me, and all the amazing "comps" in my life.

NOTES

CHAPTER ONE

4 **Christian family from Lebanon:** Lebanon's multiethnic population includes several Arab Christian denominations and a variety of Muslim sects. The civil war that broke out there in 1975 generated an exodus of nearly a million people, most of them Christians who fled to European countries and the United States. See Daniel L. Byman and Kenneth M. Pollack, *Things Fall Apart: Containing the Spillover from an Iraqi Civil War* (Washington, DC: Brookings Institution, 2007).

6 **My kindergarten teacher parked me:** Edward M. Hallowell, MD, and John J. Ratey, MD, are the coauthors of two helpful and thorough guides to attention deficit disorder: *Driven to Distraction: Recognizing and Coping with Attention Deficit Disorder*, revised and updated (New York: Random House, 2011), and *Answers to Distraction*, revised and updated (New York: Random House, 2010). Needless to say, what's considered appropriate for managing attention-deficit kids has changed a lot since my kindergarten teacher parked me behind a cardboard box!

CHAPTER THREE

27 **"We all get our own bag":** At a July 27, 2013, panel promoting his new NBC sitcom, actor Michael J. Fox—who was diagnosed with Parkinson's disease in 1991—said, "The reality of Parkinson's is that sometimes it's frustrating and sometimes it's funny. I need to look at it that way. I think we all get our own bag of hammers. We all get our own Parkinson's. We all get our own thing." Aly Weisman, "Michael J. Fox: 'We All Have Our Own Parkinson's,' NBC Show Will Portray Disease as 'Frustrating and Funny,'" Business Insider, July 29, 2013, www.businessinsider.com /the-michael-j-fox-show-will-make-parkinsons-funny-2013-7.

31 **ownership of their outcomes:** In 1966, psychologist Julian Rotter published his famous Internal-External (I-E) scale to test what people believe about who or what controls the key events in their lives. Rotter observed that people with an internal locus of control—those with a strong sense of control over their own behaviors and outcomes—fare much better than those who think events are caused by external factors such as other people, random chance, or the government. J. B. Rotter, "Generalized Expectancies for Internal Versus External Control of Reinforcement," *Psychological Monographs: General and Applied* 80, no. 1 (1966): 1–28. A large body of research supports Rotter's findings across a wide variety of populations. See Sean Robson, "Psychological Fitness Constructs and Measures," chap. 3 in *Psychological Fitness and Resilience: A Review of Relevant Constructs, Measures, and Links to Well-Being* (Santa Monica, CA: RAND Corporation, 2014). One important offshoot of this research is the Multidimensional Health Locus of Control Scale that is excerpted in the self-test for Chapter Three (see appendix, page 199). Introduced in the 1970s, this scale is now used around the world to measure people's beliefs about who or what controls their health status.

See Barbara S. Wallston, Kenneth A. Wallston, Gordon D. Kaplan, and Shirley A. Maides, "Development and Validation of the Health Locus of Control (HLC) Scale," *Journal of Consulting and Clinical Psychology* 44, no. 4 (1975): 580–585, and the website of one of the test's developers, Kenneth A. Wallston, PhD, "Multidimensional Health Locus of Control [MHLC] Scales," Vanderbilt School of Nursing, https://nursing .vanderbilt.edu/projects/wallstonk/index.php.

CHAPTER FOUR

40 **"after-repaired value":** Terms commonly used by people in the house-flipping business appear in the first five chapters of *The Business of Flipping Homes*, by William Bronchick and Robert Dahlstrom (Dallas, TX: BenBella Books, 2017).

45 **"healthy envy":** Professors Neils van de Ven, Marcel Zeelenberg, and Rik Pieters differentiate "benign envy" from "malicious envy" in their journal article, "Leveling Up and Down: The Experience of Benign and Malicious Envy," *Emotion* 9, no. 3 (June 2009): 419–420.

CHAPTER FIVE

57 **temperament, abilities, and passions:** Psychologist and neuroscientist Robert Ornstein (1942–2018), who was affiliated with the University of California Medical Center and Stanford University, described the basic dimensions of individual temperament as "set points." These set points are present in each of us from birth, but in many ways our brains can also adapt to our environment. Ornstein published more than twenty books on the brain, mind, and consciousness, including the classic study *The Psychology of Consciousness*, 4th ed. (Los Altos, CA: Malor Books, 2021), and *The Roots of the Self* (New York: HarperCollins, 1993).

CHAPTER SIX

74 **My initial goal:** Research findings on the "high performance cycle" appear in a journal article by professors Edwin Locke and Gary Latham titled "Building a Practically Useful Theory of Goal Setting and Task Motivation," *American Psychologist* 57, no. 9 (2002): 705–717.

85 **"growth mindset":** The concepts of "fixed mindset" and "growth mindset," fundamental to this chapter (and my life!), come out of the groundbreaking research that Stanford psychologist Carol Dweck and her colleagues have been doing for the past thirty years. Dr. Dweck's impact is felt in fields as diverse as education, political science, international diplomacy, and business management, and her findings are cited in hundreds of research articles. Whether they know her name or not, it is safe to say that a generation of researchers, teachers, coaches, and businesspeople have been influenced by Carol Dweck. Her best-selling book is *Mindset: The New Psychology of Success*, updated ed. (New York: Random House, 2016 [2006]).

85 **neuroplasticity:** The brain's ability to adapt and change, including forming new neurons—is now a widely accepted finding. Brain adaptations occur throughout our lives in response to an enormous number of factors, such as physical activity, learning, and environmental enrichment. See Eberhard Fuchs and Gabriele Flügge, "Adult Neuroplasticity: More Than 40 Years of Research," *Journal of Neural Plasticity*, article 541870 (2014).

90 **"in the zone":** In his classic book *Flow: The Psychology of Optimal Experience* (New York: Harper and Row, 1990), psychologist Mihaly Csikszentmihalyi uses the term "flow" to describe the profound shift in consciousness that occurs during episodes of absorbed and focused yet

seemingly effortless proficiency. The necessary condition for flow is "engagement": the focused use of our predominant strengths. See Martin E. P. Seligman, "Can Happiness Be Taught?" *Daedalus* 133, no. 2 (Spring 2004): 80–87.

CHAPTER EIGHT

110 **spring of 2007:** The news media captured the disaster in the housing market in snippets like this one, from the June 16, 2008, issue of the *Orange County Register*: "Banks foreclosed on a record 1,131 houses and condos in Orange County in May—the first time the total topped 1,000 in a month.... May's total was up 26 percent from April and *310 percent from a year earlier*" (italics added).

120 **fire in the Santa Ana Canyon:** The Freeway Complex Fire in November 2008 was one of the largest wildland fires ever to strike Orange County. Driven by fierce Santa Ana winds, the fire hopscotched from Corona through the Santa Ana Canyon, destroying nearly four hundred homes. At the Cascades apartment community alone, sixty units in six buildings were damaged or destroyed, leaving dozens of families homeless. Orange County Fire Authority, "After Action Freeway Complex Fire," November 15, 2008, www.ocfamedia.org/_uploads/PDF/fcfaar .pdf; "Freeway Complex Fire: 40 Percent Contained; 28,889 Acres," NBC Los Angeles, November 15, 2008, www.nbclosangeles.com/news/brush -fire-shuts-down-freeway-in-corona/2096266; "Apartments Destroyed by Wildfire Reopen," *Orange County Register*, July 1, 2010, www.ocregister .com/2010/07/01/apartments-destroyed-by-wildfire-reopen-2.

CHAPTER TEN

148 **"Everybody has a plan":** Alternate versions of the Mike Tyson quote have appeared over the years. The one cited here appears to originate with

Dave Lance, "Bull's-Eye Squarely on Hawks' Backs," *Dayton (OH) Daily News*, February 25, 2004, C1. Another version has Tyson saying, "Everybody has plans until they get hit for the first time," in "Biggs Has Plans for Tyson," *Oroville (CA) Mercury-Register*, August 19, 1987, 1B.

EPILOGUE

192 **"I don't wanna be":** "One Man Band" lyrics © 2018 Words & Music, a division of Big Deal Music Group.

APPENDIX

200 **Multidimensional Health Locus of Control (MHLC) Scale:** For more information, see the website of one of the test's developers, Kenneth A. Wallston, PhD, titled "Multidimensional Health Locus of Control [MHLC] Scales," available at Vanderbilt School of Nursing, https://nursing.vanderbilt.edu/projects/wallstonk/index.php.

207 **"being in the zone":** Mihaly Csikszentmihalyi, *Flow: The Psychology of Optimal Experience* (New York: Harper & Row, 1990).

ABOUT THE AUTHOR

Tarek El Moussa, self-made celebrity real estate investor, appears on a string of hit HGTV shows—*Flip or Flop, Flipping 101 with Tarek El Moussa*, and *The Flipping El Moussas*—that teach others the real estate investment business so they can build wealth and achieve happiness through success.

Born into an immigrant family in Long Beach, California, Tarek learned from his hardworking parents the value of perseverance and of pushing himself to ever higher limits. At the age of twenty, he received his real estate license. He left college to pursue real estate full time and quickly made a name for himself in Orange County, California, becoming one of the top agents in his company. By twenty-two he had purchased his first million-dollar home. Four years later, thanks to the Great Recession, he was back in an apartment and had zero dollars to his name.

In the years since then, Tarek has powered through an economic recession, a high-profile divorce, and two bouts with cancer. Financial, physical, and emotional struggles have not slowed Tarek down.

Today, Tarek enjoys a massive online and onscreen presence, with almost three million engaged social media followers and a worldwide TV audience of one hundred million. He has successfully flipped more than eight hundred properties over the years and is a successful entrepreneur, real estate expert, and investor, with a portfolio that includes more than two hundred properties; a wholesale and fix-and-flip real estate company called Tarek Buys Houses; a private real estate investment firm, TEM Capital, that focuses on commercial real estate opportunities nationwide; and a real estate education program, Homeschooled by Tarek, that showcases his expertise and teaches people to do what Tarek does. He also has a real estate team of over 1,400 agents selling across the nation. Tarek's newest company, Soar Energy, is in the green energy space.

As a two-time cancer survivor, today cancer-free, Tarek now donates his time and energy to a number of cancer-focused charities, bringing awareness and aid to those in need. Tarek's number-one priority is being a hands-on dad and spending time with his wife, Heather Rae El Moussa; his daughter, Taylor; and his two sons, Brayden and Tristan. Tarek and Heather live in Newport Beach, California, where they plan on raising their family and creating lifelong memories.